SHEHLA MASOOD

Hemender Sharma is a journalist with over twenty years of experience in print and broadcast media. Currently, he heads *India Today*'s Madhya Pradesh bureau.

SHEHLA MASOOD

THE MURDER THAT SHOOK THE NATION

HEMENDER SHARMA

HarperCollins *Publishers* India

First published in India in 2019 by
HarperCollins *Publishers*
Building No 10, Tower A, 4th Floor, DLF Cyber City, Phase II,
Gurugram – 122002
www.harpercollins.co.in

1 2 3 4 5 6 7 8 9 10

P-ISBN: 978-93-5302-963-0
E-ISBN: 978-93-5302-964-7

Typeset in 11/15.2 Stempel Garamond at
Manipal Digital Systems, Manipal

In loving memory of my father, Mr JL Sharma,
who taught me to smile in the face of adversity

Contents

Introduction

If an urban woman with modern sophistication and a questioning attitude is killed in modern-day India, the investigations begin with a close examination of her character. If the victim happens to be young, single and beautiful, her 'character' precedes all narratives, with even the motive behind the murder taking a backseat.

Shehla Masood was one such feisty woman. Leisurely stepping out of her house in upmarket Bhopal, she was shot at from point-blank range in broad daylight and killed on 16 August 2011.

Shehla's murder instantly became national headlines and was covered extensively, down to the minutest details, for months on end. She found ways to occupy media space while alive as well, organizing events that made headlines, exposing corruption through her RTI activism and becoming a tiger conservationist too. All the good press, however, ended with her cold-blooded murder.

Shehla's life was as much an open book as her telephone directory was a closed mystery. She was courageous – some would say audacious – and had a heart of gold. Open about her relationships and never afraid of who she was, her family and friends often turned to her in times of need. And Shehla wasn't one to disappoint.

She came from a humble background, but her convent education, coupled with her instincts, made her a savvy Muslim girl. She also dared to dream big.

This is the story of the circumstances that led to Shehla's murder, the politics that subsequently unfolded around the case, and the fight for justice for her – a process in which a few spirited individuals joined hands.

After her death, all sort of canards were spread about her, or found their way into the public domain. None of those stories had any basis, nor were they attributed to anyone. However, they changed the narrative. And Shehla's character was touted by the gossips as well as the press to be one of the many reasons for her murder. All this was part of a larger conspiracy by the system – which included members of the ruling political party, police and the media – to malign a woman who wasn't there to defend herself and to waylay the investigations. As the investigations progressed, the wheat was eventually separated from the chaff and the truth emerged. But the damage had been done. Her family had to undergo much pain and anguish due to the constant mud-slinging that was unleashed through the media.

As an activist, Shehla had taken up cudgels against the high and mighty. So whenever the question of her murder was posed, a dozen possibilities sprang up. And the fear of the investigation coming to a standstill haunted those who wanted to know the truth. This book is an attempt to unravel the naked truth.

All characters in the book are real, though some names have been changed.

Darbar is an important character in the story, and draws his name from his past. Another important character is Savan Bhado, who derives his name from the entry for him in Shehla's phone book. Shehla had the habit of inventing her own names for people close to her. She had concealed the identity of some people in her phone list and Savan Bhado was one of them.

The identity of two important characters, Big Boss and Auntie, have been concealed because of the nature of their jobs. The names of a few other characters that are in the CBI charge sheet as witnesses have also been changed to protect their identity.

The book also details how the CBI team, lead by Joint Director Keshav Kumar and DIG Arun Bothra, painstakingly reached the killers and how the killers tried to mislead the team and use the country's premier investigating agency to their own advantage instead. So here's the story behind the story of Shehla Masood's deadly murder.

One

The Murder

16 August 2011

The phone rang at 12.07 p.m. It was Auntie on the line, 'Just check out why Darbar has got Shehla Masood killed.' Her voice was firm. 'She has been shot outside her house. She is dead. I'm sorry,' she said.

Auntie was in Delhi at the time and was the first police officer to find out about the murder. Earlier, her call to the senior superintendent of police (SSP) of Bhopal had abruptly ended his weekly Tuesday public hearing. A deputy superintendent of police posted with the city crime branch had also been tipped off by her. By the time the police control room flashed the murder message, most of the senior officers were on their way to the crime spot, and Auntie, while sitting in Delhi, had already tossed Darbar's name as a possible suspect.

The nature of the desk she handled at the police headquarters was to keep a tab on anything associated with political power.

For those who envied her prominent postings, Auntie was always an interesting subject. Her single status came in handy for gossipmongers, who often linked her name with political men sitting in positions of authority. Irrespective of who rose or fell in the pyramid of power, Auntie had a knack of being on the right side of those who ruled Madhya Pradesh and was a mini power centre herself.

A call from this 'mini power centre' could not be taken lightly. I was at the Yadgarey Shahajani Park in downtown Bhopal, where gas victims had organized a demonstration, supporting Anna Hazare's India Against Corruption campaign.

The mood was enthusiastic all around – the bonding between the protestors and the cameramen was visible. Both sides knew what the other was looking for. It was a perfect photo session in progress.

I walked past an old lady carrying a placard in her raised hands. A picture of the corpses of two babies lying next to each other was neatly pasted on it. The handwritten caption read: 'We want justice'. The picture offered a peek into what might have happened on the deadly December night twenty-six years ago, when methyl isocyanide leaked from the Union Carbide factory in Bhopal.

Outside, on the main road, everything was normal. SSP Adarsh Katiyar's phone was continuously busy. The only way to get through to him was to just keep trying his phone. Finally, he picked up the call and without waiting for a question, said, 'Yes, it is true. Shehla Masood was found dead inside her car outside her house. She had just left her house when the incident happened. There is a bullet injury. No one saw anything. We are trying to find out more.'

But then why had Auntie taken Darbar's name? Auntie knew Shehla well. She also knew Darbar well. She perhaps had an idea about what was going on between the two, and the authority with which she named Darbar made it difficult to not believe her. Auntie's job profile included spying in the name of national interest. National interest automatically got translated into the interest of the ruling elite and Darbar, a son of a former chief minister, was certainly part of it. So, was Shehla killed because of some elite power game? Not having any basis or evidence to name Darbar, I refrained from using the info that Auntie had given me. Auntie, my source for over eleven years, had never supplied any false or factually incorrect information, but still, it was impossible to use what she had disclosed.

CNN-IBN was the first channel to flash the news: 'Shehla Masood, an RTI activist and Madhya Pradesh convener of Anna Hazare's India Against Corruption campaign, shot dead by unidentified assailants outside her house in Bhopal'.

On the way to the crime scene I called up Deshdeep Saxena, a senior journalist. We decided to meet at Shehla's house. By now, all TV crews based in Bhopal had started moving towards the crime scene.

Almost every photo and video journalist in Bhopal knew Shehla from her event management days. She ran an event management company called Miracles. It was a one-man show – at her 400-square-feet first-floor office in MP Nagar that she had taken from a close associate of Darbar, she conceptualized and planned her events. Everything was hired when required. A sofa that could seat three people was placed right behind her chair. On a square glass table attached to the wall, by the window side, rested a phone, with an Airtel connection. In one corner, a floor-to-ceiling bookshelf was fitted, while a poster of Shah Rukh Khan occupied a prominent place. The workstation included an L-shaped wooden structure with maroon upholstery covered by glass; both sides of the workstation were fixed to a wall. One side of the wall had a large clipboard, while on the other were racks into which she stuffed all her important files. Every time she needed a file or wanted to put it back, she would shout out to Irshad, her office attendant, who would get a chair from outside into this small room, climb onto it and do the job. All the important numbers in the city were pinned onto a soft board.

A printer was attached to her computer while a seven-channel music system with speakers hung on the walls. On the main glass door, a laminated paper with MIRACLES written in red, green and yellow was stuck with tape. At the bottom of the page was written: 'We make it happen'. It was here, in this office that Shehla transformed from an event manager into an RTI activist, crusader and animal rights activist.

The police had cordoned off the entire crime scene area. Shehla was lying on the seat next to the driver's seat in her Santro; her head was bent towards the left. She was dressed in a blue kurta and red salwar.

Within the house, Masood Sultan, Shehla's father, had thrown himself on a cot lying right next to the main door. Hands spread apart, he helplessly pushed at the air and screamed every time he saw someone entering the room, 'Meri bachchi ko maar diya (they have killed my little one)!' Shehla's cousin, Arsh, was crying himself hoarse. The khalas (maternal aunts) wailed. Everyone ran in and out of the house, calling out, 'Shallu, where are you?'

Outside the house, the open area meant for a park was overcrowded by now. People living in the slums next to the open area were jostling for space, trying to figure out what was happening inside the house. Television cameramen and photographers were pushing and yelling, trying to capture as much as they could. A policeman standing near the car was shouting at everyone, trying to keep people at a safe distance from the body. A lady police officer was about to search Shehla's body and asked the photographers to move out of the way. None obliged and she kept on requesting them to move.

The inspector general of police (IG), Shailendra Shrivastava, was on the phone. SSP Adarsh Katiyar was on his walkie-talkie. Both were walking in opposite directions within the area cordoned off from the public. SP Yogesh Chaudhary was overseeing the search inside the car. There, television journalists were clamouring for a sound bite from the IG and the SSP. Both Shrivastava and Katiyar obliged. All around, people stood in small groups discussing the murder and floating all possible theories. There was a commotion each time someone important arrived at the scene.

The moment DGP SK Raut arrived on the spot along with state intelligence chief Rishi Kumar Shukla, it was clear that Shehla's was no ordinary murder. The two senior-most police officers of the state saw the crime scene and went into a huddle inside the house. They spoke to Masood Sultan. Within five minutes they left the spot. By this time, Deshdeep had arrived and I told him how I came to know about the murder and how Auntie had made a pointed reference towards Darbar. Auntie was known to both of us; there was no reason for us to disbelieve her. We talked about the possible motive. There was none that we could think of.

Ayesha Masood, Shehla's younger sister, called from the USA: 'Please take control of things.' She was on my Facebook friend list and had taken my number from my info page. Ayesha was composed, but I could feel her helplessness. Sitting in a distant land, she could do nothing but make frantic telephone calls. This was only the second time that I was speaking with her.

The first time I spoke to her was on 14 August 2007. Shehla had called me at around 4.30 a.m., crying. I was at the hospital within the next fifteen minutes. The previous night I had gone to the hospital at around eight. Shehla's mother was ill and on the ventilator in a private room at the hospital. Shehla sat quietly in one corner. For the last forty days, Shehla had been cooking a liquid diet for her mother. They fought every day, as her mother resisted eating, but Shehla coaxed her like a little girl and eventually won every day. But today, it was not to be. She had not eaten anything throughout the day and Shehla looked very worried. She looked helpless for the first time since I had known her.

I left the hospital after her mamu (mother's brother) arrived, and tried to comfort her, saying that everything would be all right. Deep inside, both of us knew that nothing was going right for her mother. The end came at around 2.30 a.m. with only Shehla by her side. Shehla waited for over two hours before calling me. I headed straight to the hospital. On the way to the room, I saw Shehla's mamu, who was on the phone. Just outside the room, Shehla was standing with Ayesha, who was carrying her fourteen-day-old son Mustafa in her arms. Her daughter, Hiba, held her khala's hand.

In her other hand, Shehla carried a bag that contained her mother's belongings. The two sisters had already started planning their mother's funeral. Shehla's mother wanted things done in a certain manner after her death. I drove them back to their house in Koh-e-fiza. Shehla sat next to me in the passenger seat, while Ayesha and her kids sat in the rear seat. On the way back, I spoke about the inevitability of death. Ayesha spoke just once, 'Why does it have to happen to us?'

At the scene of the crime, my crew took all the relevant sound bites and shots. They knew I was engrossed somewhere else. I tried to focus on what I would say in my piece to camera (PTC), when my phone rang again. It was Big Boss on the other side. He enquired about what was happening on the spot and who the killers could be. I was clueless, but I asked him if I could meet him in person. The meeting was fixed for the next day.

Just about a week before Shehla's murder took place, I was with Big Boss at his office when Shehla's name cropped up. He had received a certain input about Shehla which was factually incorrect. 'Savan Bhado and Shehla have travelled together abroad and he has gifted a flat to her in New Delhi,' he said, knowing fully well that I would react and blurt out the facts.

'As far as I know, she stays in a flat on Hanuman Road in Delhi and it has not been gifted to her by anyone. It belongs to a friend of Savan Bhado. Savan Bhado also stays in the same flat along with his mother and Shehla.'

'And what about his wife?' he further asked.

'According to Shehla, she stays at the government flat that has been allotted to Savan Bhado by virtue of his being a member of the Rajya Sabha,' I said.

Savan Bhado was the spokesperson of a national political party, and his movements were being watched by intelligence agencies. Big Boss knew that I knew Shehla well. Perhaps this was the reason why he had called me today and had agreed to give me an audience the next day. Big Boss' work profile was similar to that of Auntie's, but his purview was much wider and so was his access. If he so desired, he could easily reach the prime minister of the country. The channel for this was in place.

So why was everyone so hassled by the murder of this girl called Shehla Masood, who had only recently taken a few baby steps into RTI activism? Why did the Madhya Pradesh DGP and intelligence chief feel the need to visit the murder scene of a girl who, as the MP convener of Anna Hazare's India Against Corruption campaign, had turned off all established activists with her brash ways? For during Anna's first fast for the Jan Lokpal Bill, Shehla had put up campaign hoardings across the city in which her own photograph was bigger than Anna Hazare's. How many murder scenes had the state DGP himself visited in his entire tenure?

How did Auntie, sitting in all the way off in Delhi come to know about the murder before anyone else in Bhopal?

I decided to first write the script and then return to the spot to do a PTC later. Shehla's body was removed from the crime scene and taken to the Gandhi Medical College for a post-mortem.

At the Gandhi Medical College, Dr Neelam was the doctor on duty in the mortuary. She had already performed five post-mortems since the morning. News of the sensational murder in broad daylight had already reached the hospital. At around 2.00 p.m. a constable from the Hamidia post arrived and met the duty doctor. The body was still lying in the mortuary van outside. Dr Neelam asked for the requisition slip, but the policeman refused, saying that Dr Barkul, the head of the medico-legal department of the hospital, had decided to perform the post-mortem himself. Dr Neelam left the mortuary and met Dr Geeta upstairs. Dr Geeta and Dr Neelam later decided to go back to the mortuary out of sheer curiosity. The entire city was already talking about the sensational murder.

Inside the morgue, Dr Barkul was already doing the procedure when Dr Neelam and Dr Geeta entered the morgue. As the two doctors watched him perform the post-mortem from some distance, they speculated about how the bullet could have entered the body.

Dr Barkul did not like their presence and asked them to move out. Initially they resisted, but stepped out as Dr Barkul insisted and raised his voice. The post-mortem was over in two hours. Dr Barkul signed the form after completion of the post-mortem with Dr Priyamvada, resident medical officer (RMO), forensic medicine, signing as a witness.

In the meantime, my office was chasing me for a script. While writing the story, I received a call from the input chief of a national English news channel, informing me that they had chosen me for their channel's MP Bureau. They were happy with my previous work experience and liked the interview that I had appeared in through video conferencing the previous week. The input chief was surprised at my inability to respond to the offer – he told me about the salary hike and the formality of the management interview that was yet to be scheduled, once I gave my consent. I thanked him for the offer, even as I knew that this new job, which I had been desperately trying to land, did not matter any more.

In the evening at Shehla's house, preparations were on for the burial. Her father sat in the veranda along with a few people in a semi-circle. All of them were silent. Shehla's body was lying on a cot, draped in a spotless white cloth. From her face, it appeared as if she was in deep sleep.

People came and expressed their condolences. Masood Sultan was narrating to everyone about the deadly blow that had struck him. 'Shehla had left the house at around 11.15 a.m.–11.20 a.m. I was in the bathroom shaving. She said, "Papa, I'm leaving," to which I responded with a khuda hafiz (goodbye). It must have been just five minutes after she had left when my sister-in-law came to me, shouting, "Masood miyan, please check what has happened to Shehla. She is sitting motionless in the car."'

Shehla's aunt, whom she called Bajjo, had seen her working on the computer at the dining table just ten minutes ago. She had asked Shehla when she would be leaving for work. She had ignored her aunt's question and had instead pointed at the LCD TV that she had bought just a few months back. CNN-IBN was showing live visuals from Jantar Mantar, where Anna Hazare had started his fast, demanding the Jan Lokpal Bill aimed at rooting out corruption from the Indian political and administrative system, be passed.

Bajjo had gone upstairs to her first-floor flat and started working in the kitchen. She came to the balcony after five-six minutes to check if Shehla had left for office. From the balcony, she saw that Shehla's car door was open and that she was sitting on the driver's seat with her head resting on the steering wheel. Bajjo had thought that Shehla had fainted because of weakness; she almost started scolding her niece as she walked down. It was her fifteenth roza (fast during the holy month of Ramzan) and weakness was bound to happen, as she never had her sehri (morning meal eaten before sunrise during Ramzan). For the past fourteen days, Shehla had been having just one meal and was going without a drop of water throughout the day. Weakness was bound to happen, Bajjo thought.

Masood continued, 'She went up to the car and thinking that Shehla had fallen unconscious, she rushed inside the house and informed me. I rushed to the car and shook Shehla. She was motionless. I turned back towards my house when I realized a maid was washing clothes in the adjoining house. I took water in my cupped hands from her and rushed back to the car. My world came crashing down as Shehla's dupatta slid down with the force of the water that I had thrown on her. I saw a bullet mark on her trachea. I did not remember which direction I ran and what I shouted after that. The neighbours called the police.'

A gloom of silence descended after Masood Sultan had finished narrating. The silence was broken by Darbar's arrival. He wore a greenish kurta with a white pyjama and was accompanied by three other people. I recognized two of them; one was his advocate and the second a state spokesman of a political party. Both people always accompanied Darbar on all important occasions. Darbar sat on the chair in the veranda next to Masood Sultan. It was with some effort that he was able to hold Masood Sultan's hand. I sat on the opposite side.

The house was built by Masood Sultan with his life's savings in the year 2000, two years before he retired as a librarian from the district library. While serving as a librarian, he had stayed in a government house. Masood Sultan's father had been a sub-inspector in the police department and his grandfather had migrated to Bhopal from Uttar Pradesh.

Masood Sultan did not repeat the sequence of events that he had narrated to almost every visitor, to Darbar. He regarded Darbar as a close friend of Shehla's, who had visited their house on a couple of occasions.

He asked why Darbar had not responded to the call that he had made earlier during the day. 'You were the first person I called. You picked up the phone but did not react after I gave you the tragic news. In fact, someone called Gupta called a few minutes later and told me you were in a temple.'

Darbar replied, 'I was in a temple in Ujjain.'

At around 8:00 p.m. in the evening, I received a call from a photographer friend of Shehla's. He said, 'They are trying to make it look like a suicide, a crime reporter told me. Please try and find out more. They are trying to fix Shehla's cousin for hiding the weapon.' He was crying.

I didn't believe him, but called up Shrivastava out of curiosity. He did not take my call. I then tried Katiyar. He too did not take my call. I tried calling up all the city police officers I knew. None took my call. I concluded that they must be in a meeting.

Finally, I called up Auntie and asked her to elaborate on what she had told me in the morning. She sounded evasive. I called up Deshdeep and told him what the photographer had told me. We decided that I would pick him up from his home and proceed to the graveyard where Shehla was to be buried later at night.

We were the first to reach Bara Bagh, the graveyard where Shehla was to be buried. There was ample space for parking. It had rained during the day and the narrow Sofia College Road that leads to Bara Bagh emitted a strange smell that was a cocktail of wet mud mixed with a dash of diesel left behind by mechanics and machine operators. We parked at a distance and discussed who the killers could be. Deshdeep did not rule out the possibility of the involvement of Darbar to which Auntie had pointed out earlier at 12.07 p.m. in the afternoon. Shehla's body arrived at around 11.00 p.m. We walked some distance towards the funeral procession and stood on the stairs next to a closed shop that led to someone's house in the double-storey structure. Those carrying the casket were taking very quick steps, almost running. Every eight to ten steps, the shoulders that carried the casket changed. Shehla's seventy-two-year-old father led the procession, wearing a white kurta-pyjama and a skull cap. Masood Sultan was almost running as if clearing the road ahead for his little girl. We watched the entire procession and slowly walked behind it with another common friend.

The body was first taken to a mosque outside the graveyard for janaze ki namaz (the last prayer before the burial). Inside the graveyard, the grave had already been dug. Shehla's body was kept next to the almost eight-feet–deep pit in which she was to be laid to rest. We stood at a distance and watched the rituals and waited for our turn to put a fistful of earth in the grave.

My phone's ring broke the silence in the graveyard. It was IG Shrivastava returning my call. My guess had been right. The entire police leadership had been in a huddle, discussing Shehla's murder and its possible fallouts, when I had called.

I asked him a pointed question, 'Sir, someone called me around three hours ago, informing me that the police thought it was a suicide.'

'We have registered a murder case. But we can't say anything. It can be a suicide case as well,' he responded.

'What about the weapon that Shehla had supposedly used to kill herself? Has it been recovered?' Shrivastava said that it hadn't been recovered. I tried to probe further, asking why she would want to kill herself. She was so happy.

'There could be any reason. She had cysts in her ovaries. We have registered a murder case. We have formed five teams to investigate it. But nothing, not even suicide, can be ruled out at this stage,' he said, before ending the call.

I had walked to an isolated corner of the graveyard while talking to Shrivastava. I hurried back to Deshdeep who was waiting for me. We hurriedly put a few fists of soil into her grave. On our way back to the car, while I was narrating the conversation that I had just had with IG Shrivastava, my phone rang again.

This time it was Katiyar. I asked him a straight question, 'What is this suicide theory that is being floated?' He replied that every aspect was being considered. By this time, both Deshdeep and I knew that the police were serious about the suicide theory.

'Impossible!' we said to each other. 'The cover-up has started already.'

On the way back, we spoke about life, its suddenness and unpredictability. Deshdeep called it marghat gyan – the knowledge of the circle of life that transformed Prince Siddhartha into the Great Buddha. I dropped him to his house and had driven just about two kilometres when Deshdeep called me again. The state government had released the transfer list that was already scheduled. IG Shrivastava, who had been promoted just a few weeks ago, was to be the new sports director and Mr Vijay Yadav would replace him as the new inspector general of police in Bhopal. And Yogesh Chaudhary was the new senior superintendent of police.

From now on, we had to deal with Vijay Yadav and Yogesh Chaudhary.

Two

The Life and Times of Shehla Masood

Born into a middle-class Muslim family in Bhopal, Shehla was a dreamer who dared to take risks. She knew what it took to realize one's dreams. The fact that she was a girl who belonged to a minority community in a city that was divided into two large Muslim and Hindu ghettos since the 1993 riots in which hundreds were killed – Old Bhopal and New Bhopal – meant little to her. She belonged to both the worlds of Bhopal that were divided by the majestic Upper Lake. Her house in the posh Koh-e-Fiza area, where she was gunned down, was in the old city, while her office was in New Bhopal's MP Nagar, the industrial district where opportunity thrived. Every day she fearlessly travelled between these two worlds in her silver-grey Santro, unmindful of the time of day.

Shehla was aware that she was beautiful and carefully cultivated an aura of boldness around herself. She evoked extreme reactions. To her friends and family, she was bold, kind and a go-getter who had established herself in a male-dominated set-up through sheer grit and determination. For those who worked with her, she was brash, at times ruthless, and messy with her finances. It took a lot of effort and time to get payments released from her. But the strange part was that her work never got stuck because of people unwilling to work for her. Such was her charm that she always had new people ready to do the job for her.

Unlike Auntie, Shehla was linked to just one man in Bhopal – Darbar. Her friends, however, never bothered to ask her about her association with Darbar. Sheila worked for an NGO that she and Darbar had started together. In her phone book, Shehla had saved Darbar's number under the name 'Angel'.

For her father, Masood Sultan, a retired librarian, she was equal to five sons; a daughter who took care of everything. Masood Sultan was a broken man after his wife's death in 2007. It was Shehla who took care of her father just as she had seen her mother care for him, even though she too had found it difficult to cope with her mother's loss. Wherever in the world she might be, Shehla would always call her father at least thrice a day – twice to enquire about his meals and once about his medicines. Almost a year before her murder she had shifted base to Delhi, where she was trying to set up an office, but Masood Sultan never felt as though his daughter was away. The father-daughter bonding was such that distance meant absolutely nothing.

Shehla judiciously cultivated her contacts and nurtured her friendships. She remembered the birthdays of all her friends and never missed an opportunity to organize parties for them on such occasions.

'She was benevolent. You did some little thing for her like getting someone's number and she would make you feel as if it was the most important thing in her life. She never forgot to say thanks and always remembered people who helped her,' is how an old college friend remembered her.

Her cousin Rajil, who flew in to Bhopal from Denmark, remembers the one 'thanks' that Shehla always wanted to give, but never found the person to whom she owed it to. 'When she was a little girl of about five years of age, Shehla had gone to watch a movie along with her mother and aunt in Khandwa. In those days, cinema halls had two floors; those watching the movie from the balcony had to pay slightly more than those watching from the hall on the ground floor. Shehla and her mother and aunt were on the balcony that day. During the interval, Shehla climbed onto the little railing out in the front and slipped and fell from about twenty feet. It could have been fatal, but nothing happened to her as she was caught by someone sitting in the hall below. Later, when she was older, her mother and aunt told her this incident, and Shallu Appi would often talk about the man who saved her life in the cinema hall. Shehla always wanted to meet the man to whom she owed her life, but no one knew or remembered who that person was,' Rajil recollects.

Even as a child, Shehla was very choosy, with strong likes and dislikes, remembers her aunt, Rabab Zaidi, whom Shehla fondly called 'Bajjo'. 'If she did not like something, be it food, clothes or some toy that was gifted to her, she would immediately make it known to everyone. She was not one to accept things that she did not like,' Bajjo fondly remembers. Rabab Zaidi was on the first floor of the two-storey house when Shehla was killed, and was the first one to spot her from the balcony. 'She was motionless and was leaning on the steering wheel of her car. I rushed down, went close to the car and then rushed inside the house to alert her father,' Bajjo recalls.

Bajjo is the eldest amongst seven cousins. She came to Bhopal along with her siblings in the 1960s and lived in a rented property. She picked up a job with the Education Department and while all her other siblings are married and their families are now settled in Bhopal, Bajjo chose not to marry. She was one of the first Muslim girls in Bhopal to ride a scooter (two-wheeler) to office. Bajjo was popular among her siblings and her friends and peers often talked about her courage. Family members often compared Shehla to a younger Bajjo. For the two had one thing in common – the courage to take adversity head-on. And both often emerged victorious from the various trials they encountered.

Shehla attended St. Joseph's Convent, the best girls' school in Bhopal which had a long list of illustrious alumni, the most famous being Jaya Bhaduri, the film actress who had made it big on the silver screen.

As a young girl Shehla was rough and tough and used to play football and cricket with her cousins and boys from her neighbourhood.

'After school, all of us would meet at their house. Shallu Appi would boss us around. I always felt like she was my real sister. Protective of us, she would fight for us with other boys in the neighbourhood. Once somewhere near New Market we had taken an autorickshaw. The autorickshaw driver tried to trick us and did not stop at our destination. Realizing this, Shallu Appi, even though a small girl at that time, started hitting him from the back. When he still didn't stop, she instructed all of us to jump out, and took the first leap out of the moving vehicle herself. Thankfully, the autorickshaw driver stopped after she jumped out, but she had bruises all over,' Rajil recalls.

Shehla was fond of good food and liked dressing up. She rode a scooter to BSS College in Bhopal and was an instant rage among the boys. 'She had an attitude and she knew how to carry herself,' remembers a friend.

After college, she took a degree in Mass Communication from the South Delhi Polytechnic. While doing her course, she met Sidharth Bhadoria, a Delhi-based businessman who also had a Bhopal connection. After almost a year of courtship, the two decided to get married. Initially, the marriage was kept under wraps with no one except some close friends knowing about it. The marriage ended on a bitter note, and when Shehla complained about torture – both physical and emotional – her friends had to intervene. According to a close friend, Shehla was completely shattered after her marriage failed. She had lost all hope and cursed herself for her wrong judgement. Her family never knew about this marriage and she decided to close this chapter once and for all, and returned to Bhopal in 2000.

By the time she returned to Bhopal, her father had retired and the family had shifted to Koh-e-Fiza. Shehla, after a lot of encouragement and support from close friends, started life afresh in Bhopal. Initially, she tried her hand at many jobs, including a stint reading the news at a local cable channel. Within a year or so she met Mahira, an old friend and a senior from her school. The two first came together for a fashion show that they had organized at Jehan Numa Palace in Bhopal. Mahira, who would later become an elected member of the municipal corporation, used her contacts with model coordinators in Mumbai so they could introduce the world of fashion to Bhopal in grand style. The show was called Art of Passion; perhaps reflective of the attitude that the two girls had imbibed while working in Delhi and Mumbai.

However, conservative Bhopal was not ready for this kind of fashion show at that time. The fundamentalists opposed and threatened to disrupt the event, as they believed that it was an attack on their culture. Even God was not kind to the two girls, for, on the day of the event, it rained heavily. The sponsors backed out and refused to pay the money they had promised. By then, a lot of money had already been spent on branding, and models had specially been flown down from Mumbai. According to Mahira, she had arranged for some finances, but the two parted on a bitter note after the failed venture as both had lost a huge amount of money.

It was around this time that Shehla became associated with Darbar Singh. Darbar Singh helped Shehla recover some of the money that the sponsors owed her. Later, when Shehla started her own event management company, Miracles, Darbar Singh helped her bag many contracts. Most of them were from the State Tourism department, of which he was the chairman for several years.

In public, Shehla maintained that her relationship with Darbar was limited to the work that they were doing together for the NGO, but deep inside she had already fallen for the 'Angel'. The turning point in their relationship came about in 2001, when Pakistani singer Adnan Sami of '*Lift kara de*' fame was all set to perform at a musical night in Indore. Shehla, who was to play some role in organizing the event was about to leave for Indore when she received a call from Darbar. 'I was about to leave for Indore when I got a call from an angel. He asked me to cancel the trip at any cost as a conspiracy was being hatched by one Khandelwal of a "dal" (an organization that has a national presence and is known for its anti-Muslim and anti-Valentine's Day rhetoric) to defame me or to put me in the dock at the behest of somebody. The reason is unknown. Later, I came to know that there was a protest in Indore against Adnan Sami, due to him being a Pakistani,' Shehla wrote in her diary on the day she broke up with Darbar. Shehla narrated the Adnan Sami show incident in her diary with a reference to the angel. She wrote, 'The Angel was with me for ten years but I lost him.'

One of the first project Miracles got was a Builder's Meet in 2001, in which all the prominent builders of Bhopal came together to showcase their future construction plans for the city. Miracles organized many events after this and also partnered with several newspapers, including the Bhopal-based media house, the Navbharat Group.

By 2006, Shehla had firmly established a name for herself and organized media events for almost all major product launches in Bhopal. She had also reached an understanding with RA Systems, an A-class contractor firm, under whose name she organized several big events for the cultural department. RA Systems was owned by Pramod Agnihotry, a lieutenant of Darbar Singh. But Pramod Agnihotri had nothing to do with the events; Shehla just used his name to bag the big-ticket events and executed them all on her own.

In late 2006, RA Systems was blacklisted and banned by the cultural department. Shehla had invested all her money in the events she organized for the department and had made most of the payments from her own pocket. She was expecting the payment to arrive from the cultural department, but after RA Systems was blacklisted, her payments too were blocked.

RA Systems being blacklisted was a huge blow to Shehla. She could not understand what had struck her and who was behind this decision. The reason for blacklisting the company was that the sound system provided at one of the private events organized at the Governor's house was substandard. Shehla even got an appreciation note written in her favour from the Governor's house, but the boss of the cultural department, IPS officer Pratik Shrivastava (name changed), refused to listen. Shehla knew that Pratik Shrivastava was not acting on his own. There had to be someone else behind the action taken against RA Systems. She tried to reason with Shrivastava but he refused to budge. She then applied all her resources to convince Shrivastava, who yielded to the extent that the blacklisting order was cancelled and she was allowed to participate in the next year's tendering process. Her payments, however, were not released.

As the next year's tendering process came about, Shehla participated and was the lowest bidder. But Shrivastava arbitrarily cancelled the tenders and laid down new conditions, which ensured Shehla was ineligible for the tendering process.

It was around this time that Shehla decided to take Shrivastava head-on. She complained about the injustice being meted out to her to all his superiors, but to no avail. It was then that she discovered the Right to Information Act (RTI), a tool with which she could secure her rights. She filed several RTIs in the cultural department asking for details of procedures undertaken during the tendering process. Shrivastava was annoyed and asked Shehla to withdraw all her RTIs, and warned her that he would not allow her to work with the cultural department in the future. Shehla recorded the phone call in which Shrivastava had threatened her and approached the Information Commission with a complaint. The Information Commission served a notice to Shrivastava. This was Shehla's first victory against Shrivastava, her revenge on the man who had tried to destroy her career.

Through the RTI, Shehla found out that Shrivastava had travelled abroad without taking permission from the Ministry of Personnel, a mandatory condition laid down in the rules of service for IPS officers. Realizing that this could affect his career, Shrivastava approached Shehla through common friends and a compromise was reached between the two through a mutual contact, a prominent builder of the city.

During her investigation into why Shrivastava had gone after her, Shehla found out that a lieutenant of Darbar Singh whom she trusted greatly was behind this. The matter reached Darbar, but Shehla knew that the lieutenant never did anything without Darbar's knowledge. By then, Shehla had distanced herself from Darbar Singh, although the two had never had a falling-out in public and Shehla always spoke of him with respect.

By now, Shehla wanted to give marriage another go. In 2007, one of Shehla's friends put in a matrimonial advertisement in the *Hindustan Times* newspaper on her behalf. Most of the proposals that came in response did not interest her. However, one of the suitors caught her interest. Junaid, a Bhopali settled in Pakistan, was visiting Bhopal and the two met through common friends.

Everything seemed to be working out well between them, but Shehla did not want to leave India at any cost. She had her ageing father to look after and besides, all her relatives were in India. Shehla had also become active in raising her voice against brutalities faced by women and children. People would contact her and she would often lend her voice to them and accompany them to lodge complaints at police stations. Moving to Pakistan was completely ruled out. Junaid even offered to leave Pakistan and settle in Dubai, but Shehla loved India and Bhopal too much. 'Appan to Bhopali hain. Yahan say chhod ke kahin nahin ja sakte (I'm a Bhopali. I cannot leave it and go anywhere else),' she would often say with a twinkle in her eyes that was accompanied with a high five. After a lot of wooing, Junaid finally returned to Pakistan.

Her family, too, arranged a few meetings with prospective grooms, but things did not work out. Shehla wanted to settle down, but she was fiercely independent. She guarded her independence with a great amount of caution and refused any alliance that she thought could infringe upon it.

By now she was a busy activist, and her event management work suffered a lot, with the company doing only occasional product launches. She started her blog 'Letz change d rulz', in which she started venting her feelings and reactions to anything and everything. It was as if she was in desperate search for some meaning in life. She also spent a lot of time on Facebook, networking with whosoever had an opinion on anything. She also tried cultivating a reading habit and read a lot on the Internet. She started following several blogs, including those of self-help author Paulo Coelho and journalist MJ Akbar.

It was on Facebook that she first interacted with Savan Bhado, a politician from a national political party and a regular columnist in several newspapers. With his help, she found a new passion: Tiger Conservation. She put her heart and soul into tiger conservation. She would sign off all her emails with the sentence: 'I will make sure that Madhya Pradesh remains a Tiger state'. And all her messages and status updates on social networking sites would end with a 'roar'. Meanwhile, a tigress called Jhurjhuru was killed under mysterious circumstances in the Bandhavgarh National Park. The authorities tried to hush up the matter, calling it an accident. Not convinced, Shehla started investigating the accident and found out that a minister's son had bumped off the wild cat with his vehicle at night. The tigress, according to her, had been blinded by the lights of the vehicle and she insisted it was murder, for which the staff of the national park were equally responsible. 'Why was the vehicle allowed to go inside the reserve area of the forest at night in the first place?' she asked. She held several press conferences demanding justice for Jhurjhuru and even organized a photo exhibition where photographs of the post-mortem of the tigress were shown, along with other wild-cat pictures.

After a long time, Shehla felt that she had found a cause close to her heart, and for this she gave credit to Savan Bhado.

She saw her public profile slowly change, as she started getting published for her activism. The news portal rediff.com published several articles under her name. She now wanted more and dreamt of a bigger role for herself in public life. She started working towards this and even organized a function at the chief minister's house, where she brought several thousand Muslim women to felicitate Shivraj Singh Chauhan for the work that he had initiated for the minority community. This suited both of them: with the parliamentary elections around the corner, Shivraj needed to reach out to the minority community for the Muslim vote, while Shehla was working towards a possible role for herself in the BJP in the future. On why Shehla chose the BJP, Shehla's father later said, 'She always said that the Congress used the Muslims as a vote bank and never really bothered about their development. According to her, the BJP, minus its communal politics, offered a better opportunity for the development of the common Muslim.'

In the meantime, Savan Bhado had become the national spokesperson of a political party. He had also managed to bag a Rajya Sabha nomination. But even though his professional life was going well, his personal life was a mess. Savan Bhado told Shehla about his life – how his now-estranged wife used to treat him, how she never allowed him to meet their two children, one of whom suffered from some serious ailment, and how she had tutored his daughter against him. He even showed her emails that he had written to his wife, complaining against the ill treatment.

Shehla had christened him Savan Bhado after his favourite song – '*Mere naina savan bhado, phir bhi mera man pyasa*' – the Kishore Kumar song from the film *Mehbooba* that he often sang. Shehla had even saved his number under the name 'Savan Bhado' in her phone book. Shehla, who by her own admission had lost the 'Angel' in her life, was looking for emotional support and started a relationship with Savan Bhado and shifted base to Delhi. When a friend asked her about what future she saw in the relationship, she said, 'I'm treated with a lot of respect in the family. Bhaiya, Savan Bhado's brother, and Biji, his mother, treat me with a lot of respect and we talk for hours at length. All they want is a happy life for their son and I'm happy as long as I'm treated with respect.' Savan Bhado's family wanted him to divorce his estranged wife and was working towards it. Clearly, Shehla was being fed stories about a forward-looking, liberal man being wronged by his wife.

In Delhi, Shehla got involved with the Trust managed by Savan Bhado; she organized events for the Trust in Kolkata and Srinagar, and even organized a tribal event in Dehradun.

The expenses for these events were borne by the cultural department of the Madhya Pradesh government. And those who had ousted her from the cultural department did not like this. Additionally, the fact that Shehla was building a profile and meeting top BJP leaders like LK Advani did not go well. The gang, of which Darbar alias Angel was the guiding force, swung into action and another plot to bring Shehla down started taking shape. Even though Shehla had left Darbar for good, she had not snapped all ties with him. She never imagined Darbar and his men would plot her downfall.

Shehla, with Savan Bhado's guidance, had proposed an all India Tiger Conservation Conference in Bhopal to the chief minister. The plan was to bring tiger conservationists from across the world to Bhopal. The chief minister liked the idea knowing it would bring his state into the limelight and a note was made and marked to the concerned departments. Everything was moving as per plan, and LK Advani had consented to inaugurate the conference, but the bureaucrats stalled it at the last moment. That's what Shehla initially thought, as her name figured nowhere in the final stages of planning. The conference, however, never saw the light of day.

Darbar's lieutenants were once again in the forefront, and this time they decided to hit where they knew it would hurt her the most.

An officer from the intelligence department of the Madhya Pradesh police, who is close to a top RSS functionary and its one-time spokesman, was roped in. This RSS functionary approached all senior BJP leaders, including its national chief and told them about Savan Bhado's proximity to Shehla and her role in the Trust events. The conspiracy reached its flashpoint when in the presence of Savan Bhado, this RSS functionary advised the chairman of the Trust to keep Shehla away. As evidence, he called up the officer of the Intelligence Department, who said from the other end, 'She is an ISI agent,' striking an almost fatal blow to Shehla, the liberal-thinking Muslim girl for whom India mattered more than any of those involved in the conspiracy.

Informed about this turn of events by Savan Bhado, a shattered Shehla came back to Bhopal for a brief period. She took some time to reconcile to the fact that she was being targeted because of her association with Savan Bhado. She lay low for a few days and then resolved to expose all those who were behind the vicious campaign. She met several people, including the builder who had facilitated the compromise with Pratik Shrivastava. She narrated her story to everyone who was willing to listen. She was feeling helpless and was restless. In Bhopal, she filed several more RTIs and then shifted back to Delhi hoping to re-launch the NGO, Surya (name changed).

Shehla came back to Bhopal in the second week of March 2011, this time as the convener of the Madhya Pradesh chapter of Anna Hazare's India Against Corruption campaign. Anna Hazare had already announced that he would sit on an indefinite fast, demanding the legislation of the Jan Lokpal Bill that he and his team had scripted. A lot of anger and discontent was brewing amongst the common man after the media had exposed several scams in the country.

The people who had earlier been appointed as conveners of the Madhya Pradesh chapter did not like Shehla's involvement, for they were well-aware of her brash ways, and had been miffed by an earlier stunt she had pulled off by making her photograph bigger than Anna Hazare's in a poster. However, Shehla was not deterred. She saw a huge opportunity in Anna's campaign and put her heart and soul into it. Before Shehla had been appointed the convener of the movement in MP, it had failed to take off in the state. With her enthusiasm and zeal, Shehla brought the movement into the spotlight. Her event management experience was helpful and she put everything she knew to test. She started the 'India Against Corruption Campaign – Madhya Pradesh' page on Facebook on 15 March 2011 and soon all her friends were members of the page. In no time, the page had over 2,000 members.

Throughout the day, Shehla and her group would post something or the other on the page in order to build hype around Anna's fast. A couple of days before Anna's fast started, she put up huge hoardings across the city. The word 'crusader' appeared under her own picture, which was larger than Anna Hazare's. Many in the activist fraternity in Bhopal did not like this, but there was little they could do to stop Shehla. She organized road shows and bike rallies in the run-up to the fast. When Anna sat for the fast in New Delhi, Shehla sat for a fast in Bhopal.

Shehla was back in Delhi after the Anna campaign. In the last week of June, she visited her sister in the USA, but kept a close watch on events unfolding in India. She returned from the US in mid-July and left for south India with Savan Bhado, only to be back in Bhopal in the last week of July. She then started gearing up for the next phase of the India Against Corruption campaign, which was slated for 16 August.

And then on 16 August 2011 she was shot dead outside her house. Minutes before her death, she had posted on her Facebook wall, 'Gandhi: "The purpose of civil resistance is provocation". Anna has succeeded in provoking the Govt and the Opposition. Hope he wins us freedom from corruption. Meet at 2 p.m. at Boat Club Bhopal.'

Three

The Cover-up

'Shehla ki maut: hatya ya khudkhushi (Shehla's Death: Murder or Suicide)?' screamed *Dainik Bhaskar*'s five-column headline on 17 August. The largest circulated daily in central India, however, did not attribute the suicide theory to anyone.

A murder case had already been registered at the Koh-e-Fiza police station, but top cops in off-the-record briefings pointed towards suicide. But where was the weapon with which Shehla had supposedly shot herself? *Hindustan Times* raised this question, but the cops had a ready suspect in Rahil, Shehla's cousin. Rahil had been called to the crime scene by Bajjo. At that time, he was at his house which is about a hundred metres away from the scene of the crime. As he reached Shehla's car, Shehla's father and Bajjo were crying themselves hoarse. The neighbours had already informed the police. Seeing Shehla lying motionless on the driver's seat in her Santro, his first reaction was to take her to a hospital. He shifted the body from the driver's seat to the passenger seat.

'I could not believe that she was dead. The only thing that occurred to me was to take her to the hospital. If she still had some life left in her and she could be saved. So, with great difficulty I shifted her to the passenger seat, but before I could leave the spot the police had already arrived,' Rahil had told the police.

So, Rahil became the natural prime suspect for removing the weapon of offence from the scene of the crime, once the cops had convinced themselves about it being a suicide.

The cops, however, would not allow themselves to be quoted on this. 'A murder case has been registered and investigations are on,' was the official statement given to the media. And what was the basis upon which the suicide theory was established? The cops again had a ready reference in the observations made by Dr Barkul, the chief of the medico-legal institute, who had conducted the post-mortem. The *Indian Express* spoke to Dr Barkul, who said that nothing, including suicide, could be ruled out. In the final opinion that Dr Barkul gave after the post-mortem, there was no mention of the word 'suicide'. The opinion column of the post-mortem report read: 'Death was due to cardio-respiratory failure as a result of (a) firearm injury in the neck. The firearm was discharged from contact range. The bullet recovered from the body indicates that it was fired from a countrymade gun that is (a) Katta. Duration of death was within six hours since post-mortem examination. Photographs taken.'

Realizing that no other newspaper, except *Dainik Bhaskar* and The *Indian Express* had taken the suicide bait offered by the cops, the next line of investigation was honour killing with the possible involvement of Rahil and Shehla's father, Masood Sultan.

The police started playing a dangerous communal game. The family was suspect because Shehla had been closely associated with leaders of a national political party that had at some point in time openly positioned itself against the Muslim community.

And why were the leaders of this political party not the suspects? There was no one to answer these questions.

Shehla's aunt called up one of the owners of *Dainik Bhaskar* and questioned the suicide theory being propagated by the newspaper. He promised to look into the matter.

The family realized that they were the prime suspects for the killing of their own daughter. No one said this directly, but the way Rahil was being questioned, it was quite evident. The bone of contention – how the body could be shifted from the driver's seat to the passenger seat without first taking it out; Rahil's explanation fell on deaf ears. The Koh-e-Fiza police had even started misbehaving with and harassing Shehla's cousins.

A day after her murder, Shehla Masood was deemed responsible for her own murder. The station house officer (SHO) of the Koh-e-Fiza police station openly started accusing the family members: 'Shehla's cousins Rahil and Arsh, her father Masood Sultan and uncle Sohail Akhtar are the suspects for honour killing.'

'She could have been killed because she was associated with Hindu leaders of a national political party.'

'She was of weak moral character.'

'She was a blackmailer.'

'She had links with the underworld. The passport of Abu Salem, the underworld don who was one of the accused in the Mumbai blasts, was made in Bhopal. Those who helped in making the passport are still in Bhopal.'

The Station House Officer made these accusations in front of journalists after extracting a promise that it was off-record and that he would not be quoted anywhere.

The SHO thought he was being smart by building an opinion against the dead girl and her family in the media. Neha Dixit of Headlines Today, however, recorded all his accusations against Shehla and her family through a hidden camera. The channel showed it to the entire world in the second week of October. It was clear that the police were treating the victims as the accused.

Two top cops of the Bhopal police who had received their transfer orders on the evening before paid a courtesy visit to the chief minister, Shivraj Chauhan, early morning on 17 August. The Shehla Masood murder case popped up for discussion. Both cops insisted it was a suicide and referred to the opinion given by Dr Barkul. The two officers, however, insisted that the police would get a lot of bad press and the state government would have to face a lot of embarrassment if the suicide theory was further probed. 'No one would believe us,' the two officers told the chief minister and insisted that the only way out of the mess was to order an enquiry by the Central Bureau of Investigation (CBI).

The chief minister and his aides were closely monitoring the developments. The intelligence department of the state police had already hinted towards Darbar's possible involvement. The department had been monitoring Shehla's movements and knew about her association with Savan Bhado. The ISI angle was also thrown in.

A close aide of the chief minister informed him about a letter recovered from Shehla's belongings that was addressed to the chief vigilance commissioner.

In this letter, Shehla had complained against the large-scale misappropriation of state funds by the state hospitality department that was under the direct control of the chief minister. The fourteen-page complaint mentioned BJP stalwart LK Advani's visit to Madhya Pradesh between 30 May and 2 June 2010.

Shehla had written:

> He (LK Advani) was declared a state guest on telephonic instructions received by the state protocol office from Mr Suchari, deputy secretary to the Chief Minister and a high tea was organized at the state hanger [sic] and the catering arrangements were given to Hotel Palash. A bill of Rs 17,789 was paid for the purpose by the state protocol office from the state exchequer. Mr Deepak Chopra, who is not a relative of Mr LK Advani, also accompanied him and he stayed at hotel Jehanuma Palace and a bill of Rs 13,054 was paid. Mr LK Advani visited and stayed at Pachmarhi and a bill of Rs 4,20,800 was paid for his boarding and lodging by the Madhya Pradesh State Tourism Development Corporation. A bill of Rs 54,871 was raised by the travel agency Maa Vaishnav Devi Travels for providing vehicles to Mr LK Advani and his accompanying associates. A bhoj (lunch) was also organized at the residence of the chief minister, Shivraj Singh Chauhan, on 30 May 2010 and the catering expenses were paid from the state exchequer. Bhopal Glass and Tent Store was paid Rs 14,696 for arranging tents and chairs.

The copies of the note sheets, documents and bills that Shehla had accessed under the Right to Information Act were annexed.

Shehla wrote in her complaint:

> It is relevant to mention that the visit of Mr LK Advani was his personal visit and was not at all connected with the affairs

> of the state. It is also relevant to mention that the note sheets supplied reveal that a state plane was provided to Mr Advani for his to and fro journey from New Delhi to Bhopal and a state helicopter was provided to him for his to and fro journey from Bhopal to Pachmarhi at state expenses for which he was not entitled as per law and prevailing rules.

The complaint also mentioned the double standards of the state government, which had sanctioned the charge sheet of a former protocol officer for making payments for events organized at the house of the chief minister. She reproduced one of the charges levelled against the protocol officer in her complaint: 'You have paid bills of the Rashtravadi Samajvadi Party conference and of electrification expenses incurred during various festivals and events organized at the CM House.'

Clearly, Shehla, through her RTI activism, had targeted corruption at the topmost level in the state, but the chief minister was not sure about how to deal with it. He knew that ugly questions would be posed to him if Shehla's killers were not found at the earliest. His confusion was further compounded by the suicide theory that his top cops had already floated.

Shehla's father, family members and friends were shocked by the suicide suggestion. Even those who had made a career out of solving crime refused to buy it. They had all sorts of questions for the Bhopal cops who had floated the suicide theory and had now been transferred to their new postings. Why would anyone commit suicide in a car? Why would a girl post messages on her Facebook wall about meeting people when she had already planned to commit suicide? Why not choose the isolation of a room instead of a public place right outside the house? What about the weapon? Where did it vanish? If Shehla was to shoot herself sitting inside the car, why would she put the gun to her trachea and not to her temple, which would have meant immediate and sure death?

Did the cops who floated the suicide theory ask these questions before accusing Shehla for her own death? If not: why?

Were the cops trying to cover up and save someone? If yes: who?

Could it be IPS officer Pratik Shrivastava, the former director of the cultural department? Or was it Darbar, who had close family ties with one of the top cops who had first suggested the suicide theory? Speculation was rife.

On 1 January 2010, Shehla had written to the state director general of police (DGP). The subject of the letter read: 'Police inaction on a complaint filed against an IPS officer for making threatening calls.' The second-last paragraph of the letter read: 'Also I would like to bring to your notice that I fear for my life from Mr Pratik. Also, I fear that being a powerful police officer he can implicate me in a false case.' Had her fears come true?

Shehla had posted this letter on her blog. CNN-IBN accessed the letter and reported its contents. The cops who were talking about suicide and honour killing were briefly forced into silence as the world now knew that a few months before her murder, Shehla had feared for her life because of an IPS officer and that she had expressed this fear for her life in a written complaint that she had made to the state director general of police.

Shehla had impressed Jairam Ramesh with her activism when he was the Union environment minister. On 17 August, an activist working with the gas victims told him about what the Bhopal police was up to. He was also told about the *Dainik Bhaskar* headline. Ramesh, now the Union rural development minister was enraged. He shot off a letter to the chief minister and released it to the media. The typed letter on his official letterhead read:

> My dear Shivraj Singh Ji,
> I was shocked to read of the shooting of Ms Shehla Masood in broad daylight in front of her house in Bhopal. Ms Masood had been in touch with me from time to time on wildlife conservation issues in Madhya Pradesh. She brought to my notice issues relating to Panna and Bandhavgarh and I recall having spoken to Dr Rajesh Gopal, member secretary, National Tiger Conservation Authority and Dr HS Pabla, Chief Wildlife Warden, Madhya Pradesh about her complaints. She was young and enthusiastic and I am very sad that she met an untimely end in such a brutal manner.
>
> I sincerely hope that the state government will bring the killer or killers to book soon. That is the least we owe to the memory of a committed activist.
>
> With warm personal regards.

Jairam Ramesh wrote 'My dear Shivraj Singh Ji' at the top of the letter in his own handwriting and added 'warm personal' between the typed 'with' and 'regards' at the bottom of his letter, giving an impression that he was personally hurt at the way in which the Bhopal police was trying to cover up the murder.

The chief minister did not respond to the letter, but the matter became even more of a priority for him. He did not want to take any hasty decisions. The matter was kept for discussion with his secretary, an Indian police service officer for the next day.

The next day, on 18 August, the chief minister's secretary met his boss in his office at around 9.00 a.m. The meeting lasted for about fifteen minutes. Immediately after the meeting, an Indian Administrative Service (IAS) officer of principal secretary rank, who had served in the chief minister's secretariat for over three years in the past, entered Shivraj Singh's room. The meeting lasted for over thirty minutes. Immediately after the meeting, journalists started calling each other. They were discussing what they called an udti udti khabar (unconfirmed news): The Shehla Masood murder case was being handed over to the Central Bureau of Investigation.

No one was in a position to confirm the news at that moment. Everyone said that they had heard of it, but there was no written order yet.

Around 11.30 a.m., the echoes of the Shehla Masood murder case was heard in the Indian Parliament. Moinul Hassan of the Communist Party of India (CPI) raised the topic of the murder in Zero Hour in the Rajya Sabha. While referring to the Anna Hazare campaign against corruption he said, 'When lakhs of people were on the streets protesting against corruption, an RTI activist was shot dead in Bhopal. It is a matter of grave concern. So far ten such murders have been reported and the Union government should immediately intervene to stop the murders of those who are fighting against corruption.'

Pressure was mounting on the Shivraj Singh government from all sides. The state police was also under tremendous pressure and a Special Task Force had been roped in to uncover all possible leads.

During the day, Inspector General of Police Vijay Yadav took charge from Shailendra Shrivastava. Immediately after taking charge he went to the Masood house in Koh-e-Fiza along with Yogesh Chaudhary, who had now become the senior superintendent of Bhopal police. The two officers were met with hostility. The family members initially refused to meet them. They were angry at the suicide theory that the police had floated. Yadav tried to place the blame on the newspapers, saying that the police had nothing to do with it. He said his force was investigating a murder case that had been registered on 16 August itself. From Koh-e-Fiza, Yadav went straight to the police headquarters. He met the additional director general of police, the Intelligence Department and the state director general of police and briefed them about what he had picked up about the investigations through the day.

After suicide and honour killing, it was now the turn of another theory – Shehla's involvement in a sex racket. This one too came from the Intelligence Department. 'A girl whose name started from N had been referred for a job by Shehla to a prominent builder a couple of months back. This girl was from Delhi and had event management experience. She had come to Bhopal at Shehla's insistence and had now gone missing. Shehla was after the builder to whom she had referred this girl and was enquiring about her whereabouts.' The input reached Big Boss and everyone was now trying to find out who this girl was. And who was this builder? Darbar was also a builder, but was he the one to whom the girl was referred to for a job? The inference drawn was that it was a sex racket involving high-profile builders and politicians and Shehla could have been eliminated for trying to either blackmail or trying to dig up more details.

At around 5.30 p.m. on 18 August, the phones of journalists started ringing again – this time the point of discussion was the one-line information that had officially just come out of the CM's office: Chief Minister Shivraj Singh Chauhan has decided to hand over the Shehla Masood murder case to the Central Bureau of Investigation. Within minutes, the breaking news was on all media channels.

At around 6.30 p.m., an officer from the crime branch reached the Masood house and asked Masood Sultan to formally write to the state government, requesting it to hand over the case to the CBI. Around the same time, TV journalists had gathered at the house of Uma Shankar Gupta, the state home minister, who announced to the TV cameras, 'The state government has decided to write to the CBI to take over the investigations into the Shehla Masood murder case after the family members of the dead girl requested to do so.'

The same evening, Masood Sultan was live on 'India at 9' on CNN-IBN. Rajdeep Sardesai's last question to him was: 'When the government is saying that the investigations would be handed over to the CBI, are you satisfied with this? Do you have no faith in the MP police because the names of some Members of Parliament are also coming up? Do you think that without the CBI it is not possible to get to Shehla's killers?'

To this, Masood Sultan replied:

> Listen, sir, this is a straight honest thing that I'm telling to you. My daughter on Tuesday, that is 16 August, left the house at around 11.20 a.m. saying to me that Papa I'm going. I said khuda hafiz to her. But I did not know that a professional killer hired by someone was waiting for her outside. She went outside. She opened her car and it appears to me that the killer who was waiting for her shot her as she entered the car. The sad part is that her aunt was in the upper storey of the house. She saw the car door open from the balcony. She came down rushing to me, asking me to check what had happened to Shehla. I rushed to the car and saw her motionless. In the neighbourhood, someone was filling water. I took water in both my palms and threw it on her face. As I threw water her dupatta got slightly dislocated and I saw that she had been shot at in the trachea. By that time, she was either dead or was taking her last breaths. As far as the Bhopal police is concerned, we had lots of hopes from them. But what they did was totally unjustified and biased. On the one hand, they kept on telling us that they had registered a case under Section 302 of the IPC and that it was murder, but

in their off-the-record briefings to the media they said things through which it appeared it was a case of suicide.

Seeing this plight of an aged father, Rajdeep was almost in tears and it took some effort for him to hold them back.

The same evening, the police took the two phones that were recovered from Shehla's body to a private computer software operator in MP Nagar. He was asked to copy the contact list, the dialled calls list, the incoming calls list, the missed calls list, and the received and sent text messages into an excel sheet. Shehla's cousin, Arsh, accompanied the police to the shop and while the computer operator was taking a copy, he too took a copy of everything. The police insisted that they wanted to take a copy of the hard drive in Shehla's laptop. The family insisted that the police should touch the laptop only in their presence. Arsh again was taken to the cyber cell of the district police, where everything from Shehla's laptop was copied onto a hard drive. Here again, Arsh smartly kept a copy for himself.

Shehla had stored all her pictures on her laptop. There were some recordings too. There was a separate folder for Pratik. In this folder was a recording of a telephone conversation she had with Pratik in which he asks her to withdraw all the RTI applications that she had filed in the cultural department. There were some emails that she had saved from Savan Bhado. The list of all the RTIs that she had filed was found. Pictures of the tigress Jhurjhuru's post-mortem were also found.

On her phone was the last call that she had made, the last call that she had received and the point at which she had stopped taking calls, thus suggesting a time-frame of when she was probably gunned down.

On 20 August, the family's worst fears came true yet again. Shehla's family felt that the cops were cooking up stories and planting them in newspapers. A story in a leading newspaper suggested that there was a property dispute that could have led to the murder. The English translation of the story on the newspaper's website stated:

> Even three days after the sensational broad daylight murder of social activist Shehla Masood, the Bhopal police appears to be clueless as it has failed to get any substantial lead in the case.
>
> Investigating officials, who scanned Shehla's mobile phone and laptop did not get any important information. However, the police has come across documents concerning a property deal. Shehla had recently purchased land for Rs 80 lakh and according to the officials privy to the investigation; the land deal could be the reason behind the social activist's murder.
>
> The police have now directed its probe towards finding out as to who were the other people in the land deal and from where Shehla arranged the money to buy the land.

The family was shocked to read this. Masood Sultan said that there was no property anywhere in the world in Shehla's name. And that he had bought two properties from his savings. One was the house in which the family lived and the second, a plot in the same locality and both properties were in his own name. An angry Masood Sultan called up the reporter who had filed the story, but he had no explanation to give except the fact that he was briefed by a police officer, whom he refused to name. The family feared that there was someone in the police who wanted to mislead the investigation and create an opinion against the dead girl.

The same day at 3.00 p.m., CNN-IBN telecast the telephone conversation between Shehla and Pratik, which Shehla had discreetly recorded. This was the same recording that she had submitted before the information commissioner as evidence that Pratik was threatening her.

The next day, all the news channels wanted the recording, which was readily provided to them. The focus once again had shifted to the cops and the maligning of the dead girl stopped, but only briefly.

The next disturbing story was in *Nai Dunia*, a newspaper headquartered in Indore. The story sourced from cops speculated that Shehla was murdered because she had double-crossed the banned Students Islamic Movement of India (SIMI). The story suggested that Shehla had connections with the banned outfit and that she had passed on some information to the cops that eventually led to her elimination.

I had a copy of Shehla's laptop hard drive that was in police custody. The police was planting stories against the dead girl and the only way to keep the story alive was to do stories on the RTIs that she had filed and the people who could have been exposed because of them. The state DGP meanwhile said that the role of all those against whom Shehla had filed RTIs was being looked into.

On 22 August, CNN-IBN did a story based on a letter Shehla had written to Union Environment Minister Jayanti Natarajan against illegal diamond mining in the Chhatarpur district of Madhya Pradesh.

Written on 25 July 2011, Shehla said in the letter that she was in the process of corroborating facts regarding the collector of Chhatarpur, who had allowed illegal mining. She also said that a PIL to this effect had been filed against Rio Tinto, the diamond mining company and that two collectors had been removed from the district after they refused to allow illegal mining.

Shehla had written similar letters to two MPs Anant Gangaram Geete and Jeetendra Singh Bundela.

Shehla now became an international story and representatives of the London-based *Guardian* and the *Australian Broadcast Corporation* (ABC) visited Bhopal to investigate the possible role of the company Rio Tinto in her murder.

The chief minister had requested a CBI probe on 18 August, but there was no further word on it. The state police had already started saying that it was possible that the central agency might reject the case. Friends of Darbar and Savan Bhado within their own party were getting restless. Beat reporters associated with Savan Bhado's party were tipped off about his possible questioning in connection with the murder by the Madhya Pradesh Special Task Force in Delhi.

Everyone expected the CBI to take over the case, but on 2 September, Union Home Minister P Chidambaram popped a surprise saying that no request had been received from the Madhya Pradesh government. On the same day, Madhya Pradesh Home Minister Uma Shankar Gupta countered and claimed that they had copies of the receipt of the fax message that had been sent by the state government.

Finally, on 3 September, the Union Government got its act together and late in the evening, the CBI registered a murder case against unidentified persons and took the case diary from the Koh-e-Fiza police station.

Four

The CBI Bhopal Investigation

On 5 September, at around 11.00 a.m., a team of twelve CBI officers, led by DIG Hemant Priyadarshy, reached the Masood house. The team included experts from the Central Forensic Science Laboratory (CFSL). This murder case had by this point of time assumed extraordinary hype in the media and the investigators knew that there would be immense pressure. Shehla Masood's call details somehow reached the media on the day the CBI took over the case. Among those who spoke to Shehla on 15 and 16 August were Darbar and Savan Bhado. The media now had the duration of each of the calls and television anchors asked what Shehla could have spoken about with Darbar and Savan Bhado for such long durations of time. They hinted at the suggestion that the key to solving the murder mystery lay hidden somewhere in these telephone calls. The news channels now clamoured for blood.

Twenty days after the murder, the CBI now wanted to recreate the crime scene. The crime scene pictures taken by the local police on 16 August came in handy. Local police assistance was sought for cordoning off the entire area as was done on the day of the incident.

Shehla's car, now parked alongside other compounded vehicles at the Koh-e-Fiza police station was once again brought to the spot. A thick layer of dust covered it on all sides. It appeared as if the car had been taken out of the junkyard after months and there was nothing that could be found inside it.

After parking the car as it had been parked on 16 August, CBI officials and forensic experts started searching it. They looked for evidence and found something right below the driver's seat. A CBI officer handed over this recovered item to his supervising officer. The entire team immediately got into a huddle as instructions for the safe storage of this newly recovered possession were issued. A journalist standing at the edge of the barricade watched everything. Within minutes everyone standing outside the Masood house knew something new had been recovered. No one, however, had any clue about what it could be.

The CBI team once again resumed its task as an officer hid himself behind the car. Another officer walked towards the car from inside the house. The investigators tried to recreate all possible angles from which the gunshot could have been fired.

A lady police officer of Shehla's height and roughly the same weight was made to sit in the driver's seat as if she had been shot dead. Rahil who had shifted Shehla's body was made to shift the lady officer to the adjoining seat.

The scene was recreated over five hours, but DIG Hemant Priyadarshy left the spot a little before the rest of his team. While sitting in his car he said to waiting journalists, 'It is a difficult case. No eyewitness has so far come forward. We have started our work on various angles.'

He went on to end the speculation over the item recovered from inside the car. 'It is a gold pendant and the family has confirmed that it belongs to the victim,' he said. The Bhopal police on 3 September, while handing over the case material to the CBI had also handed over a broken gold chain. The gold chain was recovered from Shehla's body and this pendant had been attached to it. A few files were also recovered from under the rear seat of the car during this search.

Questions were immediately raised over the kind of search the local police had carried out. 'If the Bhopal police could not find the pendant and the files from inside the car, how can they be expected to find the killers?' a family member said in disgust. The family for the first time felt assured that a serious attempt to get to their daughter's killers had now begun.

Among those who waited outside A-100, watching the CBI team recreate the scene of crime was Vandita Mishra, a senior journalist from the Delhi office of the *Indian Express*. She had flown into Bhopal in the morning to do a story for the Sunday edition of her newspaper. Her focus was on Shehla's life more than her murder. She spoke to Shehla's friends, family members, school and college mates, the people she worked with, the policemen who did the initial investigations, RTI activists in the city and the CBI, which had just taken over the case. DIG Hemant Priyadarshy dropped a bombshell on her, as she told him the story was meant for the Sunday edition. 'When does your Sunday newspaper go to press?'

'My deadline is Friday evening,' Vandita replied.

'In that case, please check with me before you release your story. Maybe we will have something to tell,' he said, as if the CBI by this time knew who the killers were.

Vandita told Shehla's family what she had heard from Hemant Priyadarshy. The family was now hopeful that Shehla's killers would be caught soon.

The search for eyewitnesses had also started. Masood Sultan gave a detailed statement. The domestic help who was filling water in the courtyard of the adjoining house and from whom Masood Sultan had taken water to throw on Shehla's face was the most crucial link. She had been questioned by the local police several times, but had not disclosed anything significant. A CBI inspector was specially designated to keep a watch on her movements. Deputy Superintendent of Police Bhartendar Sharma, the designated investigating officer of the case, started searching for the weapon outside the Masood house. The monsoon grass that had cropped up in an open ground in front of the house was removed. The CBI wanted to systematically rule out every possibility. The phones, laptops and other material recoveries made by the Bhopal police were also examined.

The first shocker came out on 6 September. The Bhopal police had tampered with the mobile phones of the dead girl. Their records read:

> The Bhopal police took the two phones into its possession from the scene of crime on 16 August. Her call records showed that a call was made from one of her phones at 6.46 p.m., almost six hours after she was shot dead. Calls were also made from the same phone on 17 August. Of the three calls made on 17 August, two were to a paanwalla in Mandla, while one was made to a local Bhopal number.

The tampering was widely reported by the media and the Bhopal police was left with no other option but to accept that the dead girl's phone was used while it was in police custody. However, they vehemently defended their actions and insisted that this did not amount to tampering of evidence.

The Shehla Masood murder was now being used by political parties for their own purposes. On 8 September, five days after the CBI took over the investigation, the former chief minister of Madhya Pradesh, Digvijay Singh, took a dig at the ruling party in the state, saying that its office bearers were involved in the case. He welcomed the fact that the CBI was investigating the case and suggested, 'If RTIs filed by Shehla in the past six months and the complaints made by her to the central vigilance commissioner are thoroughly looked into, the killers would be nabbed.'

The ruling party retaliated by talking about Sarla Mishra.

Sarla Mishra, a youth Congress activist, was found dead with burn injuries in her Bhopal house on 14 February 1997. Digvijay Singh was the chief minister of Madhya Pradesh at that time. Her association with politicians had led to a lot of accusations and allegations flying around, but in the end, no reason was given as to why and how she was killed.

A comparison between Shehla Masood and Sarla Mishra was inevitable. 'The end outcome will be the same,' predicted neutral observers.

On 5 September, an interview by Shehla Masood under the headline 'I fear for my life, but I will go on' in *Outlook* created further ripples in the already tense political situation in the state capital. The magazine claimed it was Shehla's last interview. In this interview, Shehla charged that she was threatened by yet another MLA from the ruling party after she had exposed corruption related to forest produce in Madhya Pradesh. She also claimed that she had blown the lid off the chief minister's expenditure on household entertainment, which ran into lakhs every month. She further asserted that she had drawn public attention towards twelve sitting judges, who according to her were involved in corruption.

In the same interview, Shehla charged Pratik Shrivastava of threatening and abusing her, asking her to withdraw the RTI applications that she had filed in the cultural department.

On their part, *Outlook* had decided to do a story on whistle-blowers and the threats that they faced just a few weeks before Shehla was murdered. They had done interviews with various activists, but Shehla's interview had been dropped at the last moment. The magazine realized the potential of the interview after she was dead and decided to carry it as her last interview. The interview provided a new dimension to the ongoing investigations and the investigators could not afford to ignore the charges that Shehla had made.

Vandita Mishra's full-page story titled 'The Life and Death of Shehla Masood' was delayed by a week and appeared in the 18 September issue of the *Sunday Indian Express*. She called up DIG Hemant Priyadarshy on Friday, 16 September, exactly one week after she was supposed to call him. Priyadarshy had nothing to offer and on the same evening, exactly one month after the murder, the CBI announced a reward of Rs 5 lakhs to anyone who could provide clues about the murder.

With not one eyewitness, no one having heard the gunshot and no one having seen the accused fleeing, the mobile phone call details became the police's most crucial possession.

Shehla used to carry two phones and both had been recovered from her bag by the police.

Shehla did not use her Delhi number on the day of her murder. There were no dialled or received calls on this number on 16 August. Darbar had called this number at around 11.28 a.m., but she was already dead by that time. His call was registered as a missed call. The previous day, on 15 August, Shehla had made two calls from her Delhi number: the first was at 6.13 p.m. and the second call was made at 7.21 p.m. – both had been made to Darbar. The first call lasted for fifteen seconds, while the second call lasted for a little over half an hour. The same day, at 8.40 p.m. and 9.14 p.m., she received calls from two different numbers that were not saved in her phone book. The first call lasted for around two-and-a-half minutes, while the second call lasted for thirty-eight seconds.

Shehla's Bhopal number, however, was active since 8.00 a.m. on 16 August. There were three missed calls on her phone; the first from a television news reporter at 7.56 a.m., and two other missed calls at around 8.35 and 8.36 a.m. from India Against Corruption (IAC) activists. She woke up to receive a call at around 8.39 a.m. from a city-based India Against Corruption (IAC) activist. Later, at 9.22 a.m. she received a call from Savan Bhado and they spoke for a little less than five minutes. The first outgoing call from this number was made at 9.34 a.m. to the television reporter who had called her earlier.

The last incoming call was at 11.09 a.m. from a number that was saved under 'Art of Living'. The call lasted for thirty-nine seconds.

Shehla last spoke to her office attendant, Irshad, at around 11.14 a.m. and the call lasted for eighteen seconds.

At about 11.19 a.m. Shehla's associate, Arpit, called her, but she did not take the call. At 11.41 a.m., Bhopal's Senior Superintendent of Police Adarsh Katiyar, who had already been informed about her murder by then, tried calling her number.

From the call details, the CBI had zeroed down on the time of the murder. She had been killed sometime after 11.15 a.m. The killers had waited for her to come out of her house, fired a single shot and fled the spot. What baffled the CBI sleuths the most was why no one had heard the gunshot. Also, the fact that

Darbar had tried to reach her ten minutes after she was dead raised several questions. Did he know that Shehla was dead or was it just a routine call? There was only one missed call from his number and that too was on 11 June, about three months before she was killed.

Darbar was a sitting MLA and the CBI did not want to take any chances.

The process of searching for witnesses started all over again. The maid from whom Shehla's father had taken water was questioned all over again. The CBI suspected that she was hiding something. She was promised money and property, but she maintained that she had seen nothing. 'I had gone to drop a container of water at my house about twenty-five metres from the spot,' she said. She also confirmed that she had heard nothing.

The neighbours were questioned next. The CBI hoped that something fruitful could be gleaned from their statements since Shehla's family had at some point informed the investigators that, immediately after the incident, the son of one of their neighbours claimed to have seen a motorcycle, but had retracted his statement after someone in his family pulled him back. The CBI tried to reach out to the boy and his parents, but no one was willing to talk.

The CBI had planted informers in the locality; they were asked to keep their eyes and ears open and their mouths shut. Their main job was to report whatever was being discussed about the murder. Occasionally, these informers would instigate a discussion on the topic and report whatever came out to their handlers in the CBI.

The names of two youths who lived in the slums came up in one such discussion. On the day of the murder, they had gone to get their television set repaired at a shop in Koh-e-Fiza. Word had spread in the slums that the two were smoking in the open ground outside Shehla's house around the time of the murder and that they had informed people in the slums that they had seen the accused fire the gunshot. The two were caught hold of with the help of the owner of the television repair shop, but they too denied seeing anything to the CBI.

Next came the turn of a vegetable vendor who sold vegetables from his hand-pulled cart. He had been seen moving about in the locality that day. Additionally, a green seasonal vegetable, kundru, was also recovered from Shehla's car. He was questioned, but he too denied seeing anything.

In private, the CBI officers now started thinking that the case could only be cracked by getting to the killers first. For this they needed some description about the killers, which could then be matched with known criminals. Details about the movement of hardened criminals in Bhopal and neighbouring areas were also gathered.

Chotoo, the domestic help working for Shehla's aunt, Bajjo, was also a suspect. He had been the first to see her lying motionless in the car. A CBI officer told the family, 'Chotoo has some idea about the killers. We have come to know that he spoke with someone about the murder.'

Chotoo's education was financed by Bajjo, and every day after completing the household work, he left for school at around 10.00 a.m. On 16 August he had not left the house till 11.00 a.m. CBI officers spent a lot of time talking to Chotoo and asked other family members to talk to him in private and tell them whatever he knew. Family members insisted that the officers were wasting their time, but in the absence of any concrete lead there was nothing much that the CBI officers could offer except come up with new theories every day.

The family members were growing increasingly frustrated with each passing day. They needed closure and the CBI had little to offer except foolish theories that were being propagated in the absence of anything concrete. The effect was especially beginning to show on Shehla's father, who just wanted to know who killed his daughter.

'A fruit vendor who probably saw Shehla's killers flee the spot has been threatened by some motorcycle-borne youths and was asked not to move around in the area. The fruit vendor has now gone missing and we are looking for him. Once he is located we are hoping to find those who threatened him, who in turn could lead us to the killers,' an excited CBI inspector, who kept watch around the victim's house, told the family one day.

Such information would bring some hope, but eventually the family stopped believing in what junior officers of the CBI told them.

The family would ask about the progress made in the investigations and the possibility of Shehla's RTI activism somehow being the cause of her murder. The standard CBI reply was, 'We are looking into the information she had sought and the information that she had already accessed, but so far it doesn't appear that she either had any information or was in the process of getting any such information that could have led to her killing.' Moreover, the senior officers could not be accessed and when they were reached with some difficulty, they would say that they had some leads but could not disclose them. The reason always offered was that the killers might get alerted.

In all this, Darbar's role was becoming more mysterious with every passing day. His missed call to Shehla's number ten minutes after the murder and Auntie's assertion within less than an hour that he could be behind the killing firmly pointed a finger of suspicion towards him. And now came another piece of evidence that showed he was trying to hide something. People from Darbar's party began floating the information that he had not gone to Ujjain on 16 August. His car had been seen around the city by several people and he had been seen moving about in an agitated state at the state party office. Shehla's father passed on this information to the CBI, asking why Darbar had lied to him about his Ujjain visit when he had, in fact, been in Bhopal that day.

The CBI again came up with its standard response, 'We are looking into everything.'

A protocol officer with the government of Madhya Pradesh, who had earlier been charged with corruption, called up a close Masood family associate – a friend of Rajil's – one day. Shehla, through her RTI activism, had accessed documents that had proven that he had been framed in the corruption case. He had received this information from his lawyer, who had been assisting Shehla in filing a complaint with the central vigilance commissioner. The complaint was regarding misappropriation of public funds during Advani's Madhya Pradesh visit. The protocol officer wanted to repay her by passing on some information.

Shehla's cousin Rajil fixed a meeting with him. They met on a busy highway and the officer narrated how he had come to know about Shehla's murder: 'I was in the secretariat when I came to know that Shehla Masood had been shot dead. I immediately called up my lawyer who had introduced me to her. After sharing with him what I had heard I decided to go to his office immediately. I was sitting with him in his office, when an office attendant came and told the advocate that Darbar had come and that he wanted to see him immediately. He asked the attendant to call Darbar inside his office, but the attendant insisted that he go out as Darbar was in a rush and had asked him to come out and see him. The advocate immediately got up from his seat and went to meet him outside. Outside, I saw that a black sports utility vehicle was parked near the main gate.'

On the day of the murder, people had seen a black luxury car moving around near the victim's house as well. This information had been gathered by the local police and published in local newspapers.

In the evening, when Darbar had visited Shehla's house, he had been accompanied by the same advocate and another friend of his.

The family passed on this information to the CBI and confronted the investigators with the question: 'Why has Darbar not been questioned? And if he has been questioned what has he said?' Again, the CBI did not divulge anything.

Meanwhile, a 'Justice for Shehla' page on Facebook that had been started on 6 September was gaining momentum and now had more than 2,000 likes. Friends of Shehla and those who wanted justice for her regularly posted their anguish on this page. Anand Sharma, an engineer settled in the US, was one of the most active members on the page. Whenever information related to the Shehla Masood murder investigation appeared on the Internet, Anand immediately shared it on the page. Anand, along with two others, Ritesh Singh from IIT Kharagpur and Avnish Singh, a technology entrepreneur started RTI Anonymous (RTIA). Through this they proposed to file RTIs for those who wanted to remain anonymous. Ritesh and Shehla had initially conceptualized RTI Leaks, where they wanted to put together all the exposés that came out from the RTI. Through RTI Anonymous, which was put through a website called getup4change.org that drew inspiration from petition website change.org, Anand Sharma initiated a petition to expedite investigations into Shehla's murder and to initiate action against police officers who had initially tried to mislead the investigations. Whosoever signed the petition received an automated reply from the CBI:

> CBI is sincerely pursuing investigation into the alleged murder of MS SHEHLA MASOOD. Due to the need of maintaining confidentiality, at this stage of investigation, we are constrained not to share day-to-day progress of investigation with the media and public at large.
>
> Hemant Priyadarshy
> DIG, CBI
> BHOPAL

The real shocker came when Anand posted his conversation with CBI DIG Hemant Priyadarshy. 'I had a talk with Mr Hemant Priyadarshy. He has requested that we close this petition. Please let me know if you all agree. As per your response, we will take the right action.' Anand, while quoting Hemant Priyadarshy, said that the messages that were generated by change.org went to the Indian president, the PMO, the home minister and the CBI director. All the messages in turn were forwarded to the CBI Bhopal unit, which was spending a lot of time dealing with them. Anand also forwarded the written message that he had received from Hemant Priyadarshy. However, the fact of the matter was that the CBI Bhopal unit had to do absolutely nothing while dealing with these messages. The reply was an automated one and did not require any effort from the CBI personnel.

However, the CBI Bhopal unit was still clueless. When everything else failed, the CBI started questioning Shehla's contacts in her phone book. One by one, all those who were in regular touch with her were summoned to the CBI office.

The standard questions posed were: 'How and when did you come to know about the murder? What was your first reaction after you heard that Shehla had been murdered? For how long did you know Shehla? Do you remember the first time you met her? Who, according to you, could have killed her and why?' The most emphasis was laid on the last question, hoping that a clue would come from somewhere.

All those who were summoned to the CBI office spoke about what they knew about the murder and the majority preferred to stay quiet with regard to the last question. Those who chose to answer the last question had nothing new to offer. Finally, it all came down to the theories that had been circulating following the murder. And once again, the Bhopal CBI started searching for the mysterious girl whose name started with N and who had allegedly gone missing. According to the CBI, the girl held the key to the case. Help was also sought from the State Intelligence Department, but it did not help in taking the investigation forward.

The Bhopal CBI, which had started the process of eliminating suspects by questioning people close to Shehla, ended up creating more confusion. Everyone was a suspect at the beginning of the investigation and by the end of the first week of October there was no clear direction in which the investigation was heading.

Darbar and his friends were also questioned. He was confronted with Masood Sultan's statement. Darbar accepted that he had lied to Masood Sultan about his presence in Ujjain on 16 August. When asked about the reason, he stated that his relationship with Shehla was such that he did not want to be on the spot immediately after the incident. The CBI was more or less convinced with what Darbar said. The investigations had once again come a full circle and there was no hope either for the family or for the investigators.

Big Boss, however, was not convinced with what the Bhopal unit of the CBI was saying. He was still firm on what he had said a couple of days after the murder. 'It was a meticulously planned, perfectly executed murder in which chances of some personal vendetta appear more likely than anything else,' he had said. He did not name any suspects, but said that it had to be someone from either the ruling party or its other branches.

Through his own channels, Big Boss conveyed his suspicion to the very top in Delhi. The message reached the CBI director, who was now all the more worried that his team in Bhopal had not delivered anything. He decided to send the joint director of CBI, Alok Pateria, to Bhopal.

Pateria, an IPS officer from the MP cadre, now on deputation with the CBI, knew Bhopal well as he had served at various important positions in Madhya Pradesh. He reached Bhopal on Monday, 10 October 2011. His brief was to find out why the Bhopal unit was not able to get any evidence when everyone else seemed to know so much about the case.

Pateria was briefed by Hemant Priyadarshy and his team. He assessed the work that was done by the Bhopal unit and returned to Delhi the next day. But before returning to Delhi, Pateria talked to his own sources too and so before leaving for Delhi he had clarity about how the case should move forward.

In Delhi, the CBI director did not take much time to make up his mind after he had received the detailed briefing from Pateria. He knew he had to put the best men at his disposal for the job. And on 2 November, in walked the man considered to be the father of forensics science in India, Joint Director Keshav Kumar and his trusted deputy, DIG Arun Bothra.

The team already working on the case was initially sceptical about this, for they felt that they had already worked a lot on the case and that they were just a step away from cracking it. The day Kumar and Bothra took charge, an inspector working on the case said on the condition of anonymity, 'I don't know what will happen to the case. I don't know who all will be in the team now. All I know is that we all had worked really hard on the case and it was just a matter of time.'

Five

The Two Rock Stars

The Arera Colony office of the Central Bureau of Investigation in Bhopal is right behind the posh Bittan Market. The market and the CBI office are on the edge of Char Imli, a small hill that houses most of the top ministers and bureaucrats of the city, along with some high-profile journalists who occupy government bungalows. Across the road, right opposite the CBI office is the entrance of Ekant Park, a garden that was set up during the '90s for the bureaucrats and ministers to clear their lungs every morning. Every day while going to office and returning home, I used to take this road that separated the CBI office and Ekant Park.

The Bhopal unit of the CBI specialized in anti-corruption cases. Before Shehla's murder, whenever a murder investigation was passed on to the CBI, a team from Lucknow had come to investigate. This was the first murder case the Bhopal CBI team was tackling. The intent and hard work were present, but the experience was lacking. They sounded their anti-corruption informers for tip-offs and one of them introduced me to Azad, a middle-rung officer in the CBI. Azad needed someone who had access to the local cops and also someone who could get him information on the people who were in touch with Shehla.

It was a convenient arrangement – I needed dope on the progress and direction in which the investigation was heading and so was ready to share whatever information I could lay my hands on with him. Often we would meet at Bittan market and at times he would call me inside the CBI office, where I was made to wait in the lobby right opposite the reception. The receptionist, an old man, knew me by my face and would gesture at me to wait in the lobby while he informed Azad about my arrival.

The investigators operated from the first-floor office at the extreme end. It belonged to Bhartendar Sharma. Azad was one of the investigators on the case and was part of the brainstorming that happened in Sharma's office.

On the early morning of 2 November, I was at the police headquarters. An additional director general (ADG) rank officer told me his theory about the reason why the Bhopal police had wanted to convert the murder into a suicide on the first day itself. He pointed towards Darbar's possible role, his business dealings and his partnership in various land investments with a senior police officer in the Bhopal force. He wanted me to do a story with this angle. I did not assure anything, saying that approval would have to come from the head office – I also wanted to show him that the information he had just passed on did not merit a news story.

I called up Azad as I drove out of the headquarters. I told him that I had something very important to share with him, something I could not discuss over the phone. Azad knew this was my tactic to meet him in person. He knew that I would bombard him with my questions and try to get some idea about where the investigations were heading. But today he was generous. He asked me to come over to his office before driving home in the evening. No specific time was fixed.

At around 7.00 p.m., I was sitting in the lobby of the CBI building. The receptionist had tried to inform Azad about my arrival but he was not at his desk. In fact, he was nowhere to be seen. There was tension in the air; I could feel it. The receptionist sat with his eyes focused on something, trying to make a show that he was busy. Every five to six minutes, a middle-aged man wearing a half-sleeved Nehru jacket walked past the reception. He was constantly on his mobile phone, battling with poor network. On several occasions, I heard him say, 'Hello, I'm DIG Bothra from the CBI.' I tried hard to figure out who he was trying to contact, but I could not figure it out.

I had been in the lobby for nearly an hour when Azad finally appeared. We walked across the CBI lawns to the extreme end from where we could see the traffic on the main road outside. We shared a smoke as I told him what I had heard at the police headquarters earlier. He told me that a team had arrived from Delhi to take over the case before we bid each other goodbye.

I reached home and was just settling down for dinner when my phone rang. It was an anonymous number. At first I decided not to take the call and return it after dinner, but then decided to take the call.

'Hello, Sharma saab, I'm DIG Arun Bothra from the CBI. I have just come to Bhopal today to investigate the Shehla Masood murder,' said a firm voice from the other side. I told him that I already knew about his arrival. He asked me if it was possible to meet him. I was delighted at his offer and asked him for a convenient time for the next day. 'Is it possible for us to meet right now over dinner?' he asked. I said yes at once. He asked me to come outside the CBI office and gave a short physical description of himself, which I did not require.

At around 9.00 p.m. I was again outside the CBI office. I introduced myself to Mr Arun Bothra outside the main gate and the first thing that he asked me was where we could eat good vegetarian food.

He sat next to me on the passenger seat while I drove to MP Nagar to 'Bapu ki Kutiya', a restaurant about 500 metres from Shehla 's office. On the way, he told me that he too had worked as a journalist for a national daily before joining the Indian police service.

At the restaurant there was a long queue for a table. We booked a table for two and asked the man at the counter to inform us once a table was available and moved outside into the open area. We stood in a far corner. Arun wanted to know everything that I knew about Shehla and the people associated with her and how I came to know about the murder.

I started my account from 16 August, 12.07 p.m., when I received the call from Auntie and her mention of Darbar's involvement and the events that subsequently unfolded. In between, I spoke about the kind of girl Shehla was and the person I knew her to be. Just then, the waiter signalled that a table was available.

We had dinner and by the time we reached the CBI office I knew that Bothra meant business. He took me to the first floor of the CBI office and introduced me to Mr Keshav Kumar, the joint director, who had taken over as the supervising officer on the Shehla Masood murder case. He was going through some papers while a technician was fixing a computer for him. It was past midnight and as I bid Bothra goodbye, I could not resist asking the question, 'Sir, what do you think about the case?'

'In the next three-four days we would be able to tell you how much time we will take to get to the killers. But we will get them for sure,' he said.

While driving back, I reflected upon the conversation I had had. I realized that I was the one who had done most of the talking, but I got the vibe that they would be the ones to crack the case.

Early the next day, I was back on my computer, googling Arun Bothra and Keshav Kumar. I called up friends in Delhi who covered the CBI. I called up the journalists whose names Bothra had mentioned during dinner. By late evening on 3 November, I had a fair idea about who these two cops were and what they had done in the past.

The stories of Keshav Kumar and Arun Bothra travelled along with them. They together headed the second special crime unit of the CBI in Delhi. The most difficult cases were handed over to them, and they were the last ray of hope for Shehla Masood's family. If they failed to crack the case, there was nowhere else to go. The Shehla Masood case had already reached the top investigators of the country beyond whom there was no one.

Getting into the elite special crime branch of the Central Bureau of Investigation was no mean achievement. An impeccable past record was required to get there. While he was the additional commissioner of the Ahmedabad police, Keshav Kumar had ensured registration of a case in the sensational Bijal Joshi gang rape and suicide case that had rocked Ahmedabad and captured national headlines in 2003 and 2004.

Twenty-four-year-old Bijal Joshi had been lured into Ahmedabad's Ashoka hotel by her boyfriend Sajal Jain, a Delhi-based businessman on 31 December 2003 on the pretext of celebrating New Year's Eve. Bijal was gang-raped by Sajal Jain and his friends, who also mercilessly beat her up and stubbed cigarettes on her before she was dumped on the road after midnight.

The police initially did not register the case when the victim had approached them. The policemen, who were supposed to arrest the accused, questioned her character by asking her questions like why she was at the hotel with a married man and his friends in the first place. All the accused were rich and powerful and had allegedly tried to grease many a palm before Keshav Kumar got involved in the case. He reportedly reached the police station and ensured that a case was registered on Bijal's complaint after her medical examination was done.

Bijal committed suicide on 7 January 2004, further complicating the case for the Ahmedabad police. The charge sheet was filed and Keshav Kumar and his team got a conviction for the five accused, including Sajal Jain, who were sentenced to life imprisonment. Seven others accused in the case were charged with the destruction of evidence but were acquitted by the court.

Kumar also had a Madhya Pradesh connection. He, as the inspector general of the crime investigation department of the Gujarat police had led a team that had arrested twenty-one persons of the notorious Pardhi tribe for poaching six lions from the Gir forest in 2007.

All the twenty-one accused were convicted by the Junagadh court and the highlight of the investigation was the fact that there was no evidence available initially. The incident had created quite a stir in Gujarat with the then chief minister of the state, Narendra Modi, rushing to Sasan in Gir to take stock of the situation.

The story goes that the police had recovered an empty matchbox with the brand name 'Ghora' from the spot. It was later found that such a matchbox was only available in Madhya Pradesh. All the accused arrested by the police belonged to Khandwa, Panna and Hoshangabad districts of Madhya Pradesh, and Kumar and his team had camped in the state for months together. Crucial evidence, including the claws of the lion, which ultimately led to the conviction, was recovered from the Pardhi women who had hidden them in their private parts.

Arun Bothra too had his own legend. He was not one to come under any kind of political influence or pressure. The *Statesman* newspaper carried a report at the time when Arun Bothra served as the SP of district Kendrapara, Orissa.

> Kendrapara SP, Mr Arun Bothra, has reportedly sought a transfer, protesting against political interference in matters of law-enforcement. Sources in the state police headquarters said the SP had written a letter to the director general of police, taking strong exception to the political interference in day-to-day affairs of police administration in the district. Earlier, a senior police official of DSP rank was transferred from here, allegedly on political grounds. The officer had invited the wrath of local ruling party leaders as he arrested two police officials close to them, under the instruction of the SP.
>
> While one of the two accused police officers allegedly forced a group of protesters to drink urine in custody, the other had allegedly lathi-charged villagers. Non-bailable warrants had been pending against the officers since last eight months.

While serving at Kendrapara, Bothra also put an end to the crime syndicate run by the deadly Tito gang. Nine members of the gang were arrested by his team. Tito's rival Hyder along with his other gang members had been arrested earlier and this brought an end to the bloody gang war in the coastal region that had claimed more than a dozen lives.

Bothra commanded the respect of the people in Kendrapara and business once again flourished. A local newspaper reported Bothra's method of policing: 'The SP has issued orders that the common man can roam around at any hour and that criminals are not allowed even during daytime.' The city observed a bandh (strike) when Bothra was unceremoniously transferred for refusing to come under political pressure and was replaced by a junior officer.

Bothra first teamed up with Kumar while investigating the Gyaneshwari train derailment case in which 148 people were killed. The Mumbai-bound Gyaneshwari Express ran off the tracks between Sardiha and Khemasuli railway stations near Jhargram in West Bengal in May 2010. The pandrol clips that fix the rails to the sleepers had been removed by saboteurs and a freight train coming from the opposite direction had rammed into the derailed coaches.

Kumar had just moved into the CBI and this was one of his first major assignments for the agency. Bothra, too, had joined as superintendent at the CBI's special crime branch in Kolkata. Keshav Kumar and Arun Bothra formed a formidable team and after staying on the railway tracks for over forty-five days, their team arrested seventeen members of the pro-Maoist Tribal People's Committee Against Police Atrocities (PCAPA). The CBI filed a charge sheet against twenty-three accused in the case and concluded that the PCAPA, backed by the Communist Party of India-Maoist (CPI-Maoist), hatched the entire plan to protest against the deployment of joint forces in the area.

The PCAPA had been demanding the withdrawal of the joint forces from the area for their alleged atrocities on the local people, but as the government did not pay any heed to their demand, the accused persons chalked out the sabotage to take revenge.

Later, the two also teamed up to investigate the 7 January carnage at Netai in the Maoist hotbed of Lalgarh in West Bengal. Here, they concluded that the Maoists had nothing to do with the carnage that had left nine people, including four women, dead and twenty-eight others injured. In the end, their team arrested twelve people, all of whom were associated with the Communist Party of India Marxist (CPIM) and the charge sheet mentioned the names of eight other CPIM associates who had been evading arrests.

In both the Gyaneshwari and Netai cases, the CBI had relied heavily on forensic evidence, and Keshav Kumar and Arun Bothra had shown how they succeeded as a team.

This team was now in Bhopal to investigate the Shehla Masood murder.

Six

The Theory of Elimination

It was 11 a.m. on 3 November when Keshav Kumar and Arun Bothra were at the Madhya Pradesh police headquarters in Bhopal. They met the director general of police, SK Raut and intelligence chief, Rishi Kumar Shukla. Contrary to initial expectations, the core CBI team investigating the Shehla Masood murder case was not touched. Bhartendar Sharma was still the investigating officer on the case. And Azad was still there along with the rest of the team. Only the supervising officers had changed. Keshav Kumar took over from DIG Hemant Priyadarshy and Arun Bothra replaced SP Yatindra Koyal.

The two CBI officers briefed the top MP cops about the progress in the case and emphasized upon them the seriousness with which the CBI was taking the case. The MP police in turn tipped off the two CBI officers about a possible call girl racket.

According to the theory propagated by the MP police, 'Darbar and his friends were fond of all good things, including women. Shehla got models to Bhopal in the guise of organizing fashion shows and introduced the girls to Darbar and his gang. She was probably killed because she tried to blackmail either Darbar or some other member of the gang.' The CBI team took the input seriously and asked for evidence, but the state police did not share anything.

Kumar had already reviewed the investigations done by the Bhopal CBI unit. 'What was the basis on which the MP police presumed within a couple of hours of the murder that Darbar could be involved? Where did this intelligence input come from and what was its basis?' he asked the local unit. There was no definite answer given to this question, but the presumption prevailed that the MP police somehow knew that Darbar and Shehla were in touch and they probably also knew what they had been talking about. Kumar consulted Bothra and shot off a letter to the MP police asking a straight question, 'Was Shehla Masood under surveillance? Were her phones being tapped? If yes, please make available the findings,' he wrote.

Even if Shehla's phones were being tapped, it was done discreetly in the name of national interest and no formal permission from the concerned authorities was taken. The MP intelligence department was uncomfortable with this order and Kumar's letter was construed as interference.

DGP SK Raut was roped in and he spoke to the CBI director, complaining against Kumar. The CBI director pulled up Kumar for asking such questions.

The relationship between the MP police and the CBI team started to wither from this point and reached a flashpoint in a meeting that was convened by the state DGP. The meeting was called to discuss the way forward. Over a dozen officers, all high-ranking, attended the meeting. Kumar had requested for the meeting and the agenda was, 'How the MP police could help the CBI nab the killers of Shehla Masood'.

The meeting lost significance when an inspector general of the Bhopal police spoke out, 'The Shehla Masood case is not my priority, my hands are full.' Both Kumar and Bothra looked at each other and then towards the DGP. The DGP looked away and did not say a word. After this there was no official interaction between the CBI and the MP police on the Shehla Masood murder case.

The review of the investigation done by the Bhopal unit of the CBI had thrown up Darbar's name. He was the number one suspect. He had already been questioned and the movement of his close associates, many of whom had a criminal record, was under watch.

Again, Darbar was questioned about Masood Sultan's claim that he had lied about being in Ujjain at the time of the murder. Darbar accepted his lies. But why did he do so? 'I'm a political figure. Shehla was known to me and I did not want to be seen there at that time. I asked my friend Gupta to call Masood Sultan and tell him that I was in a temple,' he told the CBI.

The Bhopal CBI had questioned Gupta as well. In his statement, Gupta accepted that Darbar was a friend from his schooldays, 'I received a call from Darbar on 16 August. He asked me to inform Masood Sultan about being at the temple and I did the same for my friend.' Gupta also disclosed that he had heard Darbar talking to Shehla at his Vidya Nagar office on 15 August at around 7.00 p.m. 'He was asking Shehla to join a political party where she felt comfortable,' he said.

Darbar's lawyer friend Mishra, his political representative Pandey and his close associate Lunavat were also questioned. Lunavat accepted that he knew Shehla through the NGO that they had started in 2004. 'Darbar introduced Shehla to me at his office. She ran her event management company Miracles from the office that I had taken from one Shibu Thomas when he was leaving for America. Initially, the NGO was run from that office, but in 2007 it stopped its operations and I don't know how Shehla started the work of Miracles from there. I had no written agreement with her,' he said.

Lunavat also told the CBI that he had received a phone call from Darbar on 16 August. 'He told me that Shehla had been shot dead and asked me to come over to his house immediately. I reached there in fifteen to twenty minutes and there he told me that he had been informed by Shehla's father about the murder.'

Shehla's aunt Bajjo had also called Darbar, Lunavat informed the investigators. 'Darbar told me that Shehla's aunt had called to inform him that the police had not reached the spot. I immediately called up the inspector general, Shrivastava, who told me that some Masood girl had been killed. I told him that it was Shehla and that is how the police was arranged.' The CBI knew that Shrivastava was one of the officers who had propagated the suicide theory, but there was nothing available beyond this with which Lunavat could be confronted.

Lunavat helped the CBI to map out Darbar's movements throughout the day of the murder. The CBI knew this would be crucial if his connection was established with the murder at a later stage.

They first went to Lunavat's office. From there they went to Darbar's Char Imli house. The next stop was the IT minister Kailash Vijayvargiya's house, and then back to Darbar's house. In the evening, they gathered at advocate Mishra's office. Another friend Singhdeo also came to the advocate's office and from there they left for Shehla's house.

Darbar and his associates' movements were suspicious but there was no direct evidence. Phone call records of the entire gang were scanned with the hope that there would be some clue. But there was none that the CBI could get hold of.

Kumar and Bothra, for their satisfaction, started the whole process all over again. Men in plain clothes were sent to the slums right opposite the scene of the crime, where the maid from whom Masood Sultan had taken water lived. The maid was questioned yet again. She was even promised a reward with an assurance that her identity would not be revealed, only if she could remember who had stood outside Shehla's house minutes before Masood Sultan had taken water from her. She stuck to her earlier statement. She remembered nothing. There was little or almost no hope of finding an eyewitness to the crime now.

The only option left now was to go for forensic or technical evidence. Both Kumar and Bothra were convinced that if the killers had been using a mobile phone they could eventually be tracked down. But what if they had not used a mobile phone and had just shot her dead and moved out of the area? The CBI hoped that the cash reward of Rs 5 lakhs would encourage informers to come forward.

It was a long-drawn process. Two mobile towers were kept in focus. The primary focus was on the mobile tower located on the rooftop a couple of houses away from the spot of the murder. This particular tower had three sectors covering different areas and directions. Sector 1 comprised of the area to its left, Sector 2 covered the area in front of the Masood house, where the murder had been committed, and Sector 3 covered the rear side of the house which merged with the other Idgah Hills mobile tower. Over nine lakh mobile phones had moved in and out of these two towers on 16 August. The challenge was to pin down the mobile phone of the killers from among these nine lakh other mobile phones. One by one, each and every phonecall coming into these two towers on 16 August had to be systematically removed from the suspect list till the killers were eventually reached. There was, however, a big if. What if the killers had not carried a mobile phone? The CBI knew it was going to be a long way to go.

The CBI was now also contemplating increasing the reward money from Rs 5 lakhs to 10 lakhs.

And what if the killers were not amongst the nine lakh phone users who had visited the two towers that day? The CBI once again went to whoever it could and asked just one simple question, 'Who could be behind the murder and why?' A comprehensive list was made from the responses that came from various sources: intelligence agencies, MP police officials who had dealt with the case in Bhopal, Shehla's family, her friends, RTI activists, journalists, police informers, and the CBI officials who had worked on the case so far.

While Kumar started scanning the mobile tower dumps and call detail reports of various suspects, Arun Bothra got down to eliminating the suspects from the prepared list one by one.

At the top of the suspect list was the ruling political party's wing organization.

There were startling similarities between the murders of RSS pracharak Sunil Joshi and Shehla Masood. Both were shot dead from close range. Big Boss, in his assessment, had also concluded that it could be someone from either this organization or a political party who could have eliminated Shehla Masood.

The CBI investigators went through the Sunil Joshi murder case diary to find out if there were any more similarities between the two murders.

Sunil Joshi, an RSS pracharak and a suspect in the Samjhauta blast case, was shot dead from close range in Dewas in Madhya Pradesh on 29 December 2007. Initially the Madhya Pradesh police declared it a blind murder and filed an application in court for the closure of the case.

The case was, however, reopened when Sunil's name figured in the Samjhauta train blast and the ruling establishment feared it could lead to embarrassment. The Dewas police in its charge sheet filed in the case claimed that Joshi was eliminated by fellow hardliners, including Malegaon blast accused Sadhvi Pragya Singh Thakur, for his high-handedness and the fear that his arrest would unmask the role of right-wing party associates in the explosions that had rocked several parts of the country.

The 432-page charge sheet filed by the police also said that the Sadhvi was annoyed with Sunil as he had personally misbehaved with her and his overall behaviour was something not expected by a woman.

There was a similarity in the execution of the two murders, but what about the motive? 'It could be her association with Savan Bhado,' the CBI concluded.

Earlier, Savan Bhado had travelled with Shehla to Europe. The CBI was informed that he had initiated divorce proceedings against his wife and was planning to marry Shehla. He had introduced Shehla to his mother and brother and they had approved of her.

When Savan Bhado was questioned, he was confronted with these facts along with the evidence that the CBI had gathered. Savan Bhado accepted his association with Shehla. He could not deny that the two had travelled to Europe together. 'But this is my personal life and it has nothing to do with the murder,' he argued.

Savan Bhado had also convened a press conference in Delhi in which he accepted that he had a professional relationship with Shehla and had demanded justice for her. Shehla's father had also confirmed that he had received a call from Savan Bhado a couple of hours after the murder. 'He asked, is it true? I told him, yes, she has been shot dead. And he put the phone down. After that there was no communication from him,' Masood said in his statement.

Savan Bhado was confronted with the material evidence that the police had recovered from Shehla on 16 August. The report of the seizure showed that she had in possession Savan Bhado's identity card, traveller cheques, cheques issued by him to her, and even a blank cheque signed by him.

The CBI was now sure that Savan Bhado was not involved, but could Shehla have been murdered because of her involvement with him? Who was getting affected by his involvement with Shehla?

The affected parties were his wife, as he was leaving her for another woman and the organization he belonged to that had problems with Muslims. He, after all, was the national spokesman of a national party.

Savan Bhado told the investigators that with his backing, Shehla had organized events for the Shyama Prasad Mukherjee Trust. The money for these events came from the cultural department. He also said that many in the Madhya Pradesh division of the ruling party did not like Shehla working for the Shyama Prasad Mukherjee Trust and that they, with the help of an MP police intelligence officer, had tried to label her an ISI agent. The angle was getting complicated now.

And who was this intelligence officer and why did she do this?

'She had a very close relationship with a senior functionary in the political party and a former spokesman,' Savan Bhado stated.

Before moving on to this IPS officer, the CBI first sought to check upon the possibility of the involvement of Savan Bhado's wife. Her phone call records were called up but nothing came of them and she was the first to be eliminated from the list of suspects.

Next came the turn of the police intelligence officer. Her mobile phone was found in the loop that originated from a phone number from Sector 2 of the mobile tower covering the Masood house.

This number was that of Shehla's associate, Arpit. A few minutes after the murder, Arpit, who lived about a hundred metres away from Shehla's house, had called a Bhopal-based RSS activist who ran two NGOs. This RSS activist, within minutes of receiving Arpit's call, had picked up his landline and dialled the number of this intelligence officer, who at that time was in Delhi.

This officer then had called a deputy superintendent of police (DSP) of the Crime Investigation Department of the Bhopal police. The DSP was called in for questioning in Bhopal. He initially did not remember anything, but after some tough questions, he accepted, 'Yes, I was informed about the murder of Shehla Masood by an IPS officer who was in Delhi that day,' he said.

Savan Bhado had tipped the CBI about this officer's association with a senior RSS functionary, who had served as the organization's spokesman in the past. The CBI now wanted to check upon this RSS functionary, but nothing could be done in haste. The top bosses monitoring the investigations directed the field officers not to proceed in haste. After permission from the very top, the mobile call details of this RSS functionary and the intelligence officer were called up. The CBI wanted to check their respective locations at the time the call had originated in

Bhopal. 'If the two are found to be together or in touch with each other through a mobile or a landline phone at that time, the possibility of the involvement of the ruling party's organization increases,' the investigators concluded. But the two were neither together, nor in touch with each other at the time of the murder and hence the ruling party's organization was eliminated from the suspects list at this stage.

The list of calls from the mobile tower had now come down to six lakhs. The forensic team concluded, 'The killer, after pulling the gun, must have fled the spot. If the killers were carrying a mobile, their mobile phone should have left the Koh-e-Fiza tower within minutes of the murder.' The mobile dump was squeezed down further as the forensic experts concluded that the killers could not have stood outside the house since morning. 'The killers must have come into the area some hours before the murder and if they carried a mobile phone, their phone should make an entry in the tower sometime before the murder,' the forensic experts deduced. To be on the safer side, phones entering the Koh-e-Fiza tower after 8.00 a.m. and leaving the tower between 11.15 and 11.30 a.m. were now kept on the table. Despite all this, it was still a long and exhaustive list.

Through its investigations, the Bhopal unit of the CBI concluded that Shehla had political ambitions. As evidence, they found details of an event that she had organized at the chief minister's house. The event, concerning issues Muslim women faced, was under the banner of the Progressive Muslim Organization. The event was backed by a prominent builder who aimed at propping Shehla up as a prospective candidate on the ruling party's ticket from the Bhopal Central Assembly constituency. Incidentally, the builder was also close to the chief minister. The area of Bhopal Central was under Darbar and he had a lot of influence there. During her association with Darbar,

Shehla could not even get the ticket for a corporator's election and here she was being propped up as a possible candidate for the legislative assembly. Could this have annoyed Darbar?

Darbar was now one of the foremost persons of interest on the suspects list. His wife too was on the list.

And though the ruling party's wing organization had been ruled out, the CBI was yet to find the reason behind the MP police labelling Shehla an ISI agent. The whole thing had started with an anonymous complaint against Shehla and a person named Ajay Dubey, alleging that they (Ajay and Shehla) were involved in a fake currency racket.

The complaint had been filed at the IG office and the Bhopal IG had marked it to the MP Nagar police for further investigation. As a consequence, the MP Nagar police had issued a notice to Shehla and asked her to file a reply, which she never did.

Shehla had thought Pratik Shrivastava, the former cultural department boss, was behind this. She had even registered her complaint with the state DGP. The DGP asked the Bhopal IG to conduct an enquiry. The enquiry never took place.

The CBI got hold of the letter that was marked to the MP Nagar police for investigation, and so at this point, Pratik Shrivastava also came onto the CBI radar. The investigators now grappled with this question: Had someone from the MP intelligence department been working with Shrivastava to label Shehla as an ISI agent? If yes, there was a possibility that the same team could be behind her murder as well.

In the second week of November, Keshav Kumar and Arun Bothra travelled to Dewas, where the RSS pracharak Sunil Joshi had been murdered.

An informer had tipped off the CBI about a possible suspect: Sudhakar Prabhune alias Sudhakar Rao Maratha.

Sudhakar's dossier was called up and it was found that he had been in touch with Sunil Joshi and was allegedly involved in the murder of five Muslims in various parts of Madhya Pradesh and Rajasthan. He had taken to crime when he was nineteen. His name had first cropped up in the murder of Jafar Khan, who had been shot dead in Chittorgarh. Jafar had married Sudhakar's sister, Jyoti, and he was killed to allegedly 'avenge' this 'humiliation'. Another Muslim, Hanif Shah, was allegedly killed as he had married a Hindu girl, Hema Bhatnagar. The list continues, with people from the Muslim community figuring prominently on Maratha's kill list.

Shehla, too, was a Muslim and the investigators were now searching for a motive that could have annoyed Hindu fanatics. The matter got further complicated when the investigators discovered that Shehla had facilitated the marriage of a Muslim boy, Umar, with Priyanka, a Hindu girl from a family associated with the ruling party's wing organization.

In April 2007, Umar, a Bhopali youth and resident of Koh-e-Fiza, converted to Hinduism and changed his name to Umesh to marry his lady love Priyanka. The couple fled Bhopal and went to Mumbai, fearing retaliation from the girl's family. The girl's family had a strong RSS association, and registered a kidnapping case against Umar, despite both the boy and girl being adults.

The police, playing a partisan role, picked up Umar's brother Shakeel and illegally detained him in the lockup. Their solution to other family members who went to meet Shakeel in the lockup was, 'Give us Priyanka and take away Shakeel.'

Shehla was friends with Atique, Umar's eldest brother. He approached her for help and she asked him to record his meeting with Shakeel when he went to meet him in the lockup. Atique recorded his meeting with his younger brother on his mobile phone when he went to give him food the next day and passed on the video clip to Shehla. Shehla in turn passed on the video clip to the media.

Meanwhile, activists from the ruling party's wing organization staged a protest outside Umar's house. The Bhopal IG was forced to convene a press conference to say that all was well. At the press conference, he was asked a pointed question about Shakeel's illegal detention and the police playing a partisan role. The IG denied that Shakeel was illegally detained. This became a huge news story, with television channels playing Shakeel's illegal detention video and the IG's denial back to back. To add to matters, Shakeel's wife went to almost every news channel to tell her story, crying on national television pleading for her husband's release. By evening the police was forced to eat crow and Shakeel was freed.

Umar and Priyanka, meanwhile, had approached the Mumbai High Court that declared their marriage legal and asked the Mumbai police to provide protection to the couple. The Mumbai High Court asked the Bhopal police to file a reply in view of the circumstances, which further dented the image of the Bhopal police.

The story had a clear connection with the conservative wing of the ruling party, a fact that evoked CBI interest. But on further drilling it was found that Sudhakar Maratha had already been arrested by the Bhopal police on 28 September 2010.

The CBI now turned to the Muslim hardliners who were on the list of suspects. This was due to mainly one incident that happened a few days before Shehla's murder.

On 7 August, eight days before Shehla's murder, a group of Muslim youth asked a group of Muslim women to go back to their houses while they were shopping in the Chowk Bazaar.

The youth claimed they were inspired by the preaching of the city qazi (religious leader) who had advised women against shopping alone or without purdah (veil). In his sermon, Shahar Qazi Mufti Syed Fazil Qasmi had appealed to the community members to avoid sending women alone in the market for Ramzan shopping. He also advised Muslim women to go for shopping only when accompanied by a male member from the family and also asked them to wear the veil in public.

When the Muslim women in the city refused to accept this diktat, the young men went on a rampage, attacking shopkeepers with scissors and looting, which led to communal tension in the old city.

After the incident occurred, the qazi clarified that the youth had misunderstood him and that he had delivered the sermon in the light of a Hadith, a Muslim religious text, and had never asked anyone to stop women from shopping alone.

After the qazi's clarification, the communal tension eased in the city and a case of looting was registered against nine unidentified persons. Several well-meaning citizens from both communities appealed for patience and Shehla expressed her views as well. A small piece under her name was carried in the 'Letter to the Editor' column of the Bhopal edition of *Hindustan Times*. Shehla wrote that the qazi was misunderstood by the rampaging youth and that there was no such provision of banning women from shopping alone in Islam.

By that time, she was already hobnobbing with top politicians and other leaders from the right-wing organization. Her very public comment on what the qazi meant and what the provisions were in Islam could have infuriated the hardliners who had attacked the shopkeepers. The CBI thought so too and now looked at getting these men who were still unidentified.

The CBI approached the local police for help yet again. After the incident on 7 August, the Bhopal police had registered a case against nine people and had arrested two of them on 17 August, while three were arrested the next day. The remaining four were still absconding. Now CBI went about looking for the whereabouts of these four on the run. The phone numbers of the four absconders were processed through the mobile tower dump data, but they had been nowhere on the scene.

At the same time, the process of collecting telephone numbers of known criminals in and around Bhopal was slowly gathering pace. The idea was to process these numbers in the mobile tower dumps that the forensic experts were going through every day.

In the absence of any definite direction, it was now time to look at the suspects that had been drawn from the RTI applications that Shehla had filed. It was difficult to find a murder motive in Shehla's RTI applications. No apparent motive was available, but the investigators could not afford to take the risk of omitting any angle.

The Bhopal CBI unit had already scanned the RTIs that Shehla had filed in various departments. The list of applications filed and the information obtained by her under the RTI Act were found on her laptop and office computer. Once again, Bothra and Kumar scanned each and every application. Of the entire lot, only three cases were kept aside – the ones that the CBI thought had the possibility of providing a murder motive.

The first was a letter drafted by Shehla to the central vigilance commissioner in which she claimed that she had accessed information under the Right to Information Act that suggested that there were large-scale irregularities in the protocol and hospitality department of Madhya Pradesh. The letter that named top national leaders from the ruling political party was drafted by an advocate Mishra.

The second RTI was filed regarding the case of the tigress Jhurjhuru, who had allegedly been killed in a collision with a four-wheeler in the Bandhavgarh national park on 18 May 2010. The tigress was found dead in the Jhurjhuru dam on 19 May 2010 at around 9.20 a.m. It was alleged that a minister's son or nephew was involved in the entire episode. Lunavat, in his statement to the CBI on 17 October 2011, had said that Shehla had filed several RTI applications against this minister's son in connection with the Jhurjhuru killing.

The third case kept aside was that of Australian mining giant Rio Tinto's plans to mine diamonds in Chhattarpur in Madhya Pradesh. Shehla had written letters to various members of parliament and the Union environment minister, Jayanti Natarajan, in which she alleged that illegal mining was being done in Chhattarpur and that two district collectors who had opposed illegal mining had already been transferred from the district.

The CBI now realized that every angle that they had probed ultimately reached the ruling class in Madhya Pradesh and vanished into thin air all of a sudden for want of evidence.

Once again, the CBI was convinced that the killers had to be traced first and the masterminds and the motive could be taken care of later.

The timing of the murder was the most crucial aspect. The investigators knew that the closer they could get to the exact time when the trigger was pulled, the easier it would be for them to track the killers through any possible communication between them and the masterminds. Apart from recreating the crime scene, the timing of the crime was zeroed down upon through available records.

The police control room had recorded a message from Charlie 2 (the call sign for the constable on duty who moves around on a motorbike and carries a wireless radio set) at 11.36 a.m.: 'The woman is unconscious and an ambulance is required. Please inform the 108 Emergency Management Research Institute (EMRI).'

The constable had reached the scene of the crime from the Koh-e-Fiza police check post on directions from Base 73 (the call sign for the Koh-e-Fiza police station).

The police station had received a message from the control room at 11.30 a.m., 'Someone has fled after hitting a girl near Shirin Complex under the Koh-e-Fiza police station.'

The control room had relayed the message to Base 73 after receiving a call on the emergency number 100 at 11.27 a.m. The call was received by constable Usha Sen.

The ambulance called for by Charlie 2 (the constable to reach the scene first) was not required, because Vijay Dohre, the batch officer in the police control room, had recorded a call at 11.32 a.m. that he received on the police control room's landline from 108 EMRI: 'One Mr Masood's daughter, who was sitting in a car outside her house, has been shot dead by someone. Masood's house number is A-100 and it is close to Shirin Complex under the Koh-e-Fiza police station area. The girl is dead.' The ambulance was already on its way.

The duty of the two batch officers who work in every shift at the control room, is to relay the messages that they receive from various police stations and act on information that comes via the emergency number 100 and other landline numbers.

Dohre in his record also noted that he had started informing all senior officers about the incident from 11.35 a.m. onwards. The first call at 11.35 a.m. was made to Inspector General of Police Shailendra Shrivastava and the second call was made to SSP Adarsh Katiyar. The chief of the medico-legal institute, Dr Barkul was also informed on directions from the SSP.

The lady who had called the control room at 11.27 a.m. was Pushpa Jain, resident of A-98, the third house from the house directly in front of which Shehla Masood lay dead inside her car. And this was not the first call that she had made from her mobile. At 11.25.32 a.m., she had called 108 EMRI.

'Please come to Koh-e-Fiza. Someone has fired a gunshot inside the car. Right now, the person is alive,' recorded the 108 EMRI server, which records all incoming calls.

After thirteen seconds, at 11.25.45 a.m., the EMRI server recorded another call from a landline number from the address A-101. The caller, Gopi Chand, said, 'I'm calling from Koh-e-Fiza, A Sector [Sector 1]. Please send an ambulance at A-100. Someone has left after firing a gunshot at a lady sitting in the car outside A-100, Koh-e-Fiza, Housing Board Colony. Her father is crying hoarse.'

The third call recorded by the EMRI server was from a mobile number from one Mukesh at 11.26.33 a.m., who said, 'A lady has been murdered outside A-100. Someone has shot a woman on the road.'

The first caller, Pushpa Jain, had come out of her house when she heard Masood Sultan shout for help. Masood Sultan had started shouting for help the moment he saw the bullet mark on his daughter's neck. He had been informed by Shehla's aunt that she was lying motionless in the car, following which he had shaken her and brought water in his hands from the woman who had been filling water outside A-101 and thrown it on his daughter's face.

The CBI recreated the entire sequence that Masood Sultan had gone through on 16 August and estimated that it had not taken more than one minute.

Thus, it was presumed that Shehla Masood was shot at before 11.24.32 a.m.

From Shehla's mobile phone call details, the investigators knew that she had received a call at 11.11.09 a.m. from a number saved under 'Art of Living'. The call had lasted thirty-nine seconds.

Lasting just eighteen seconds, Shehla had spoken to her office attendant Irshad at 11.14.40 a.m.

At 11.19.28 a.m., Shehla's associate Arpit had tried to call her again, but she did not take the call.

The investigators now had a fair idea about the time of murder. Shehla Masood had been shot at any time between 11.15 and 11.25 a.m.

This ten-minute period was the most crucial one and all mobile phones that registered their presence between 11.10 a.m. and 11.25 a.m. on the mobile tower that covered Koh-e-Fiza were now put on the table. The list was still exhaustive and comprised of thousands of numbers.

The CBI had already concluded that the killers must have fled the spot immediately after committing the crime. From the zeroed down list, the numbers that had left the tower after 11.15 a.m. were set aside. The size of the list reduced, but it was still a huge database and what made matters worse was that there was not one number that matched with the criminal database that the CBI had so far collected.

The investigators laboriously went about eliminating numbers from this trimmed-down list. The first to be eliminated were numbers of area residents. The list slowly reduced, but there was still a lot of data to go through. Next to be set aside were numbers that came into the tower on a regular basis.

From the now shorter list, the CBI gathered numbers that had left the Koh-e-Fiza tower after 11.15 a.m. on 16 August and had not entered the tower again for the next one week. The CBI were now left with a small list of over fifteen numbers. Owners of all these numbers were now being physically verified.

On 9 February, the CBI was informed by a Bhopal police constable that a history-sheeter from the Tila Jamalpura area had tried to mislead the constable about the murderer. 'He told me that Salim Kela was involved in the killing of Shehla Masood. I tried to find out about the whereabouts of Salim Kela and found that he was lodged in the Gwalior jail,' the constable told a top CBI officer.

The numbers of this Tila Jamalpura history-sheeter were processed through the mobile tower dumps. One of his mobile numbers was found to be in touch with one of the numbers from the list of fifteen numbers that the CBI was now physically verifying. His number was also found to have been moving around in Koh-e-Fiza on 16 August.

Azad confirmed to me that some progress had been made on the case, but no further revelations could be made. The CBI was now questioning all the people who were in touch with these two numbers. Nothing more was known.

Seven

Shehla Masood Murder Cracked

On 28 February 2012, seven months and twelve days after Shehla Masood was shot dead outside her house in Bhopal, I got a call from Azad at around 4.00 p.m. He skipped the customary greetings and said, 'The case is cracked. We have just arrested the main accused. The paperwork is being done,' and he disconnected the call. I called him back, but his phone was inaccessible.

Azad had this habit of calling from various anonymous numbers. Most of them were landline numbers. I had saved all of them and tried calling them one by one – most were busy but one was picked up by a lady, who said that it was a PCO number.

On the previous Sunday, I had received a phone call from Azad after a long time. We had chatted for over fifteen minutes, but the only thing he had to say was, 'Please pray for us. We have worked really hard on this case. For over six months we have been walking, sleeping and eating this case. Hope things turn out well.' I took this as a huge hint. Never before had Azad asked me to pray and I tried to press him to be more specific, but he did not say anything further.

The next day, I sounded my office about the possibility of the Shehla Masood murder case being cracked. On Wednesday, a colleague covering the CBI beat in Delhi was tipped off. 'It appears to be a case of contract killing,' she wrote in her note. I once again called up Azad and he confirmed the contract killer theory.

About ten days before the call on 28 February from Azad, I had met Keshav Kumar at the Bhopal airport. I had gone to pick up a friend coming from Mumbai. Kumar was going to Delhi. There was an added calmness to his already composed demeanour. This time I did not ask him about what was happening with the case. 'From your composure it appears you have found something significant,' I said to him. He gave me his customary reply, 'Let's hope for the best, we are trying.'

I had heard this reply from him on as many occasions as I had met him, but this time it was different. 'Sir, you are looking calmer than your usual self. I think you have either cracked the case or you are close to cracking it,' I tried probing further, hoping to get some signal on the progress of the case. But Kumar just smiled and walked away.

On my way back from the airport I called up Arun Bothra. After several rings, he picked up the phone. I told him about my chance meeting with Kumar at the airport. 'Is there an arrest happening any time soon?' I asked him and he took a long breath and spoke after a small pause, 'We are working. You can never say anything until the killers are finally nabbed.' This again was his standard operative response to any journalistic query, but from that sigh that I heard on the phone I could sense there was a huge sense of relief in the CBI.

The signals coming from all sides in the week before 28 February had been positive. It appeared as if the case was nearing completion, but the anxiety was building as we still did not know who the killers were and why Shehla Masood was murdered.

A couple of days before I had met Kumar at the airport, CBI special director Salim Ali had come to Bhopal. His visit was kept under wraps. He went to Masood Sultan's house and tried to assure him that the killers of his daughter would be caught. No one in the media got a whiff of it. I got to know of the visit as Masood Sultan had called me after Salim Ali had left his house. The entire sequence was playing out in my head as I tried to figure out what to do next.

Azad had called me with his startling news around 4.00 p.m. and over fifteen minutes had passed by now. I was getting restless. I could not flash the news until I had more details. I tried calling him again, but in vain; the automated message was the same, 'The number that you are trying to call is either switched off or has moved out of coverage area.'

I then called up Arun Bothra. Luckily, he picked up the phone instantly. I asked him straight up, 'Is it true?

He replied, 'Yes.'

'Congrats!' I said, 'Who are the killers?' I scrambled for a pen.

'Zahida Parvez.'

'Who?'

'Yes, her name is Zahida. She is an architect. Her office is in MP Nagar zone one and she has been arrested. She hired the killers and we have arrested one more person, Shakib Ali alias Danger. He is a history-sheeter in Bhopal and he got the shooters from Kanpur. While one of the shooters, Shanoo Olanga is dead, we are looking for two others who accompanied him. We will arrest them soon.'

'How much were the shooters paid?'

'The arrests have just been made. It is still not known how much exactly the shooters got, but Zahida gave three lakhs to Shakib Ali to execute the murder,' he said.

'And why did she get Shehla killed?' I asked.

'Well, we have just arrested Zahida Parvez in Bhopal. She is yet to be questioned and the paperwork is still being done. But Shakib Ali, who got the killers for her, is saying that she told him that Shehla had an affair with her husband, Asad Parvez.'

Bothra knew that Shehla was in a relationship with Savan Bhado. I reminded him about this fact and he said, 'This is what Shakib Ali is saying. We have foolproof evidence about the execution. The motive, if it is something else, will be found, as we will now interrogate the two accused. We are hopeful that we will get the remaining two accused by late evening today.'

On 28 February, I called up Masood Sultan. He was at home. It was a normal Tuesday for him. 'The case has been cracked. CBI has arrested the two main accused. I'm sending my car, you please be ready and come to my office,' I told him. Masood Sultan wanted to know more about the killers. I said, 'I'm finding out the exact details. By the time you reach my office, I will hopefully have more details,' I said.

Next, I sent an email to my office, giving all the details that I had got from Bothra. I was not convinced about the motive that Shakib had given the CBI. I decided to say nothing about the motive in my mail.

'CBI cracks the Shehla Masood murder case.' It immediately became the lead story on CNN-IBN. Other news channels followed soon.

For the next twenty minutes, I was live via phone on CNN-IBN. I juggled with the little information that I had so far gathered. 'According to sources in the CBI, Zahida Parvez, a Bhopal-based architect got Shehla Masood killed with the help of contract killers. Zahida gave Rs 3 lakhs to a history-sheeter named Shakib Ali and he got three contract killers from Kanpur. One of the killers, identified as Shanoo Olanga, is dead, while the CBI is trying to arrest the two remaining shooters. Zahida Parvez and Shakib Ali have been arrested.'

The news anchor asked the next most obvious question, 'What was the motive?'

'The motive at this stage is not clear. The CBI is claiming that it has got foolproof evidence to nail the killers and the motive would be clear once the accused are interrogated.'

'Was it related to Shehla's RTI activism or was it something else?' was the next question.

'No, she was not killed because of her RTI activism and instead was killed because of some personal enmity. The main arrests have just been made, investigations are on to get to the actual motive,' I replied.

By the time I disconnected the call, my mobile phone had forty-seven missed calls. Most of them were from police officers and journalists. 'Who is this Zahida Parvez?' everyone wanted to know. The common question from the police officers to whom I spoke after the news broke was, 'Has the CBI made it official?' I told them whatever I knew.

I required more information on the killers now. The numbers of all my CBI contacts were either switched off or out of coverage area. I went to Facebook and keyed in Zahida Parvez. Several profiles matching the name appeared, but there was only one from Bhopal. In her personal info, she had written, 'I'm an architect based in Bhopal.' Because of her privacy settings, I could access only two of her display pictures.

The first picture was with a small girl standing behind her. In the picture she wore a black top with a green dupatta. She had an oval face and had tied her hair loosely behind her. The picture was taken in poor light and nothing more could be made out. In the second picture, she was sitting in what appeared to be her office. The blue chair on which she sat matched the colour of the wall to her right. The desk and shelves in the picture were stacked with papers. She seemed of fair complexion and was smiling in the picture.

I was looking at her profile picture when Masood Sultan came running into my office. 'Shehla was killed by hired killers and this woman hired the killers,' I told Masood Sultan, pointing at the picture on Facebook.

Masood Sultan broke down. He started crying and was trembling. His pain and anguish could be seen in his eyes.

'Do you know this woman?' I asked him.

'No, I have never seen, met or heard about her,' he said.

After crying for almost five minutes, Masood Sultan tried to regain his composure and while running both his hands over his eyes and face he asked me, 'Why did she get my child killed? What wrong had she done to her?'

I repeated the reply that I had given to the news anchor a few minutes earlier.

Next, I had a live link to my news channel, with Masood Sultan as my guest. As there was still no additional information on the case, I repeated the initial facts to our viewers and then pushed the mike before Masood Sultan. He started crying. He could barely speak and in a trembling voice said, 'I have not been informed by anyone and it is from you that I have come to know that the killers of my daughter have been nabbed. I thank the almighty for this.'

At long last, there was some closure and relief for him. For six months and eleven days, Masood Sultan had slept with the hope that the next day would bring him the news of his daughter's killers.

Television crews from various other news channels wanted to take Masood Sultan's interview and had already reached my office before the live link was over. They wanted his initial reaction, but he refused. 'I don't want to talk to anyone at this stage,' he said.

He then said to me, 'I want to stay alone for some time. I am switching my mobile off. Please drop me at my relative's house in Koh-e-Fiza. I have not properly mourned my daughter's death. I want to mourn now.'

A few minutes after Masood Sultan left my office, my phone rang again. This time it was an anonymous number. And to my pleasant surprise, I realized it was Azad. As I had guessed, his phone battery had died and there was no way he could have spoken to me. This time we spoke at length and he explained to me about the way in which the CBI had methodically collected evidence.

'A phone loop had been established. Shakib called one of the killers minutes after they had fled the crime scene. The killers confirmed that the job had been done and Shakib called up Zahida. This telephone loop helped the CBI crack the case,' Azad said.

But before signing off Azad dropped a bomb. 'Shakib walked into the CBI net after he realized that he had been cornered from all sides. His friends and relatives had already been questioned and it was a matter of time before he would have been picked up. He thought it prudent to turn an approver in the case,' he said.

I once again asked about the motive. He said, 'Shakib is saying that Zahida told him that she wanted to eliminate Shehla because she had an affair with her husband Asad Parvez. We have not questioned Zahida yet. We had no option but to arrest her and seal everything in her office. If we had first called her in for questioning, there was a great chance that her associates would have tampered with crucial evidence. At least for now, we have sealed her office and no one can touch anything over there. We had discussed it among ourselves and arrived at the conclusion that whatever evidence we will get, we will get it from her office, as Shakib had always met her at her office.

'Shakib is coming by the 7.00 p.m. flight to Bhopal. He will not be masked at the airport. You can get exclusive visuals,' Azad tipped me as he signed off.

My next destination was the Bhopal airport. The Delhi-Bhopal Indian Airlines flight was late by an hour. We reached well ahead of time. The camera was fixed at the main gate. The idea was to record the exit of each and every passenger and later figure out who Shakib was. When it was announced that the Delhi-Bhopal flight had landed, an Innova car bearing a taxi number parked itself right next to the main exit.

The passengers of the Delhi-Bhopal flight started coming out of the airport. The first one to emerge was a middle-aged man who was carrying only a handbag. He was followed by two men who were not carrying any luggage. Behind these two men walked three men of similar height. The man in the middle had a moustache and both his hands were held by the two men who walked alongside him. I knew this was Shakib Ali. The three men moved towards the waiting Innova. As the car moved out of the airport, it was joined by two more escort cars with policemen in plain clothes sitting in them.

Shakib was taken straightaway to the Bhopal CBI office, where Zahida had also arrived. Shakib was to spend the night at the CBI lockup, while Zahida was taken to the women's police station.

Heavy security was put in place outside the women's police station and no video journalist or photographer was allowed to go anywhere near the main gate.

News channels, however, had picked up Zahida's photo from her Facebook profile. A friend of Shehla's called to inform me how the story was being played out on television channels. 'They are playing her picture alongside Shehla Masood's picture and calling it a love triangle. Is it true that Shehla was killed because she had an affair with this man called Asad Parvez?' she asked.

'That's what the CBI is saying but I don't think so,' I replied.

In Delhi, top CBI officers had briefed the beat reporters about Shehla's alleged affair with Zahida's husband, which became the motive for the murder.

At CNN-IBN, the final script was being readied for the flagship bulletin show, *India at Nine*. A colleague called to inform me about the CBI Delhi input. I reasoned with them that the CBI itself did not have any idea about the actual murder motive as of now. Our story that went on air at 9.00 p.m. said, 'The murder motive is still not clear.'

Around the same time, all the way in Kanpur, Uttar Pradesh, the special task force and deputy superintendent of police, Triveni Singh, were getting restless. Singh had been roped in for help by the CBI after mobile tower dumps showed that the suspicious numbers moving in Koh-e-Fiza in Bhopal were in touch with someone from Begumganj in Kanpur. His informers in the area were on the job and he and his team had gone to Begumganj thrice earlier during the day on a wild goose chase. But before they could reach anyone, Shakib surrendered before the CBI and provided them the name of one of the killers, Irfan, and his exact address in Kanpur.

Earlier in the week, Singh had spoken to Irfan's father, but he had no clue about his son's whereabouts. 'Irfan left the house after he married a mother of two. I did not approve of this marriage and I don't know where he has gone,' he said. He, however, confirmed that Irfan came to the house to meet family members once or twice a week. Irfan had not come ever since Singh had first visited the house at the beginning of the previous week.

An STF team disguised in plain clothes kept a watch on Irfan's house in Begumganj for over one week, but Irfan did not come to his father's house. The CBI and the UP STF now thought he had given them the slip. The CBI could not wait indefinitely and was now left with no other option but to arrest Zahida.

At around 9.00 p.m., Singh got a call from his informer in Begumganj; Irfan had just entered his father's house. In twenty minutes, Singh and his team were at the spot. 'Is he still inside the house?' he asked the informer. The operation started the moment the informer confirmed Irfan was still inside his father's house.

Gunshots were exchanged from both sides and Irfan was arrested for attempted murder and for firing on the STF team. A case under the Arms Act was also slapped against him.

Someone from Singh's team had already tipped a television journalist about the operation. The same evening Irfan confessed before television cameras about his involvement in the murder.

'Yes, we killed her. We were told that she was a bad influence on girls. Shanoo Olanga pulled the trigger, while I and Salim accompanied him,' he said.

The CBI bosses were informed about the arrest. The search for Salim had just started.

Eight

The Mystery Deepens Yet Again

29 February 2012

Activity outside the women's police station started building up at around 9.00 a.m. The first to reach the spot was a camera crew from a news agency. Within minutes, the area was buzzing with more camera units from media channels. The word doing the rounds was that Zahida Parvez, who had been arrested by the CBI the previous day for her alleged involvement in the Shehla Masood case, would soon be taken to Indore where her police remand would be sought from a special CBI court. The sight of so many video journalists jostling for space attracted the attention of many passers-by.

Zahida Parvez's arrest was prominently carried out by all newspapers. The famous Bhopali batolebaaz (men who had turned gossiping into an art form) were in a state of shock. Bhopal had never seen anything like this. 'A woman hiring contract killers to eliminate another woman, that too in the holy month of Ramzan, lahaulvilakuvat, what times are these!' was the common refrain before Bhopali abuses started the conversation. No one really asked or had to be told about what was happening inside the women's police station. Everyone seemed to know that the alleged killer of Shehla Masood was inside and everyone wanted to have a glimpse. Soon police personnel from the city control room had to be called in to control the crowd and manage the smooth flow of traffic outside.

Around 9.30 a.m., I got an email notification on my mobile. It was an email from Azad. The mail carried an attachment with a photograph of two men with guns in their hands. One was sitting on a motorcycle wearing a helmet while the other stood next to the bike. The picture was a television grab that was perhaps published by some local newspaper in Kanpur. The headline at the top read, '...we are again publishing this picture after enlarging it. See page six.' On the top right-hand side of the picture was printed an exclusive. Nothing could be made out from the picture, except the fact that the two men were gun-toting criminals.

I called up Azad immediately. He said, 'This is the picture taken by a photographer outside a Kanpur court minutes after Shanoo Olanga was shot dead in a gang war.'

I asked him if the shooters had been arrested? 'That is being looked into.' I asked him if I could meet him and we fixed a meeting over breakfast.

In my meeting with Azad, I learnt that Shanoo Olanga was a known name in the contract shooting fraternity in Kanpur. He had twenty-six cases registered against him in various police stations in Kanpur. Four of them were for murder, while four were for attempt to murder, and then there were cases registered against him under the Arms Act and the Gangster Act.

A member of the dreaded D2 Gang that had carried out kidnappings, killings and extortion for over thirty years in Uttar Pradesh and even outside the state, Shanoo Olanga was at one point of time one of the gang's sharpshooters. The four cases of murder registered against him were all related to killing members of rival gangs. Ever since the gang had disintegrated, Shanoo had been living in the wild countryside.

The story of the D2 Gang, which modelled itself on Dawood Ibrahim as is suggested by its name, started somewhere in the 1980s, when one Taufiq, its first leader, was booked in a murder case in the Chamanganj police station area in Kanpur. The gang initially comprised of five brothers who indulged in various crimes. By 1981, the gang was led by another cousin of the brothers, Rafiq, who announced his arrival by killing a police informer in Kanpur. Land grabbing and contract killing were the gang's specialty and at one point the Kanpur police had seized property worth several crores belonging to them.

The D2 Gang rose to prominence after its name figured in the high-profile assassinations of Kanpur politician Shahid Iraki, advocate Kurshid Ahmed, who was pursuing a case against the gang, and Special Task Force constable Dharmendra Singh.

In the mid-'80s, the gang realized the importance of political patronage and one of the brothers, Atiq, became the vice-president of a political party.

Iqbal was the first brother to be killed in an encounter. The police came down hard on the D2 Gang after it had killed STF constable Singh on 17 August 2004. Two of its shooters were gunned down by the police and on 13 October of the same year, Taufiq, the eldest brother of the gang, was killed by the police in Kanpur.

Two other brothers, Shafiq and Afzal, are serving life imprisonment after being convicted in a murder case in the Koli Bazar area in Kanpur. Shafiq was also sentenced for a kidnapping and murder that he had committed in Pune. The brothers appealed against their convictions, but their sentences were reaffirmed by the Supreme Court of India.

The D2 head, Rafiq, was killed by members of a rival gang, who shot him in the head on 30 March 2005 when he had been guiding a police team to a safe house in Kanpur's Govind Nagar locality, where he claimed he had hidden an AK-47 rifle and a pistol. He had earlier been arrested in a raid conducted at a house in Chhota Babu Lane in Kolkata.

After Rafiq's murder, the gang was almost neutralized and only one of the brothers remained free and at large. Many of the gang's sharpshooters were killed in police encounters, but some, like Shanoo Olanga initially maintained a low profile and then started searching for work outside Kanpur. In 2006, Shanoo was involved in the killing of one Naushad Kalia in Varanasi.

On 30 November 2011, Shanoo Olanga was shot dead outside the Kanpur court premises in broad daylight. A photographer of a local newspaper had clicked the killers' photograph seconds after they had shot Shanoo Olanga dead. The picture was published by the newspaper the next day.

The FIR filed by his father Israr said that Raees Banarsi and Sharif Dapali had killed his son over an old enmity. Raees, who was involved in several criminal cases, was arrested in January 2012 in Varanasi. Police claimed that he had confessed to killing Shanoo Olanga to avenge Kalia's murder. As his accomplices, he named Sharif Dapali, Guddu Bind and Monu Pahari.

The police confirmed to the CBI that the photograph taken after the Shanoo Olanga killing and published by a local Kanpur newspaper the next day was genuine. But was the story told by

Raees Banarsi genuine or was Shanoo eliminated by those who had hired him for Shehla Masood's murder? The CBI was not in a position to rule this angle out until Shanoo's killers were questioned. Raees and Sharif were in judicial custody and their interrogation could be held, but Guddu and Monu were still at large.

The Shehla Masood murder mystery was deepening.

Irfan had already added a twist at the time of his arrest. 'Shanoo had pulled the trigger, while I and Salim accompanied him,' he had said immediately after his arrest. The twist was that he knew nothing about Salim except his name and the fact that he was an associate of Shanoo, who was now dead.

The dossiers of D2 Gang members maintained by the UP intelligence department were now being searched. But there was no Salim found in there. The Kanpur police was alerted; DSP Triveni Singh was on the job once again. At long last, one Salim with some criminal antecedents was traced to Agra. He dealt in raw leather and had some connections in Kanpur. An STF team was immediately dispatched to Agra.

Outside the women's police station, photographers and video journalists had to zoom in to get a few frames of Zahida Parvez, as she walked out of the lockup and was ushered into the waiting car just a few steps away from the main gate. She covered her face with a pink scarf and only her glasses were visible. Reporters unsuccessfully scrambled for a sound bite, as the car moved towards Indore, where she was to be produced before a special CBI court.

Immediately after Zahida was taken away, a girl appeared on the spot. This girl, with a strong build, concealed her identity by covering her face with a scarf, but was more than willing to give a sound bite to the waiting television crews. And as boom mikes were pushed towards her, she said, 'Zahida has been framed. She has nothing to do with the murder,'

'But who are you and what makes you think that Zahida has been framed by the CBI?' the waiting journalists asked.

She simply refused to give her name and started howling, 'She has been framed…'

In Indore, reporters did what their colleagues in Bhopal could not manage. They spoke to Zahida. As she walked out of the special CBI court in Indore, both her hands held by policewomen, she said, 'The CBI will have to prove what I have done. I did not know her and I had never met her.' Zahida had dropped a bombshell.

Inside the court she said, 'The CBI is attributing the murder motive to an alleged affair between Shehla Masood and my husband, Asad Parvez. He cannot have an affair with me. How will he have time for Shehla?'

Whatever she might have meant by this, the newspapers had their headline. *Patrika* quoted Zahida Parvez and reported the next day: 'The CBI is trying to suggest that my husband Asad Parvez had an affair with Shehla. This is not correct. He does not have time for me; how can he have any relationship with her?'

The CBI asked for Zahida's custody for ten days, saying that she had to be questioned to recover the vehicle she had used on 16 August to visit a particular spot in the city where she had paid the hired killers. Advocate Nafeesa Khan, who appeared on behalf of Zahida, opposed the CBI's demand saying that ten days was too long a period for recovering a vehicle. The special CBI court remanded Zahida to CBI custody till 6 March.

Shakib Danger was also presented in the special CBI court and he too was sent to CBI custody till 6 March.

The CBI was already feeling the pressure. The loop had established a connection between the killers and the identity of those who had hired them had also been established. The middleman had turned up to help the CBI; Zahida and one of the killers Irfan had been arrested. But the motive was still missing.

Zahida and Shakib Danger reached Bhopal at around 8.00 p.m. They were taken immediately to the CBI office at Arera Colony, where three officers waited for them.

Additional Superintendent of Police AGL Kaul had now joined Keshav Kumar and Arun Bothra's team. Kaul, who had earlier investigated the sensational double-murder case of teenage girl Arushi and domestic help Hemraj in Noida, was appointed the investigating officer of the Shehla Masood case almost a fortnight before the case had been cracked. He had been reluctant to take over from Bhartendar Sharma, when Shakib Danger had walked into the CBI net and Special Director Salim Ali had handed him over to Kaul. He had questioned Danger in Delhi and was one of the two men who had held Shakib's hand, as they had walked out of the Bhopal airport.

Zahida and Shakib were taken to two different rooms and Zahida's questioning started immediately.

Shakib too was questioned about the motive. He repeated his story and said, 'This is what Zahida told me. If this story is not true, she must have lied to me or she is lying now. Whatever might have been her motive, but she told me that she wanted to eliminate Shehla because she had an affair with her husband,' he said every time the question of motive cropped up.

In the other room, Zahida kept throwing tantrums. She misbehaved with whosoever went to interrogate her. There was no woman investigator with the CBI Delhi team and there was not much they could extract from Zahida. She kept on repeating, at times shouting, 'The CBI will not be able to prove anything against me. I will be out soon.'

Soon, a lady CBI officer, Rekha Sangwan, who had dealt with many hardened women criminals in the past, was specially summoned from Delhi to interrogate Zahida. The lady officer was the only hope for the CBI team to break Zahida. She was asked to reach Bhopal by the first available flight the next morning.

The investigators so far had not been able to make a profile of Zahida Parvez. She had not shown any kind of remorse and her behaviour was one of arrogance. She still thought no one could touch her and that the CBI custody was one short passing phase which would soon end.

The CBI had already tasked special teams to piece together the history and profile of all the players involved in Shehla Masood's murder and their association with each. The results were being compiled as the inputs flowed in.

Zahida Parvez

Born to middle-class parents in Gadarvara in the Narsinghpur district of Madhya Pradesh, Zahida always knew her maternal uncle (mamu) Tajammul Hussain to be her father. Tajammul Hussain and his wife did not have any children and they had adopted Zahida when she was just three years old.

Hussain lived in the Andherdeo area of the old Jabalpur city from where he also ran his hardware shop named Mullaji Hardware. He did good business and money was never an issue with the family. Zahida went to Christ Church Girls Senior Secondary School in Jabalpur, popularly known as the Christ Church School. According to her schoolmates, she was always a bright student who focused on her studies. After school, she did her graduation from a college in Mumbai. In college, she was known as being a conservative person who would always talk to people with respect.

While she was still studying, Tajammul Hussain, through a friend, found a matrimonial alliance for Zahida. Asad Parvez from Bhopal was an engineering graduate, who had done his MBA from the USA. He had then settled in Bhopal and managed his family business.

After the marriage, Zahida moved into Asad's house at Sofia College Road, where he lived with his mother and sister. The house was constructed by Sajjad Hussain, who had founded Sofia College and was popularly known as Sir Syed of Bhopal after Syed Ahmed Khan, the founder of the Aligarh Muslim University. The ownership of this palatial house is still with the Sajjad Hussain Trust.

Zahida never spoke to her neighbours. No one in her neighbourhood knew that she was an architect or an interior designer. All that people living close to her house knew was that she went out in the morning and came back in the evening every day. They all thought that she was assisting her husband Asad in the family business of property and petrol pumps. 'She appeared very arrogant and never even parked her vehicle. She would leave it on the road and someone from amongst the petrol pump staff would come and park her vehicle,' said a neighbour and member of the close-knit Bohra community to which Zahida and her family belonged.

The community has a trading history and its members own huge properties in Bhopal, including those on both sides of the Sofia College Road.

Inside the palatial house, it was a completely different story. Zahida's seventy-year-old mother-in-law, Fatima Ali, told the CBI that her daughter-in-law was a short-tempered woman and that she started misbehaving with her within months of her marriage with Asad. She even accused Zahida of trying to usurp the family property.

'Zahida has a very short temper and she often misbehaved with me. She had gone to the extent of physically pushing me on a couple of occasions, while trying to attack me,' Fatima Ali said.

Zahida also had a history of breaking household items when anger overtook her. 'She can go to any extent when angry,' her mother-in-law said. She also said that Zahida had instructed all the servants and petrol pump staff not to listen to Fatima Ali's instructions and that she had tried to humiliate both her and her daughter, Sabiha, in front of the servants.

Fatima Ali had, in fact, registered a complaint against Zahida at the Shahjahanabad police station. The entire family, including Fatima Ali, her daughter Sabiha, Asad and Zahida were summoned by the family counselling centre, but nothing came of it. Fatima Ali claimed that the police advised her to approach the court, as they could not do anything because of the pressure applied by Asad and Zahida. She, however, could never approach the court, as her husband, Yusuf Ali, had died around the same time, she claimed.

Zahida's sister-in-law Sabiha said that Zahida controlled her husband Asad completely and that she started misbehaving with her some months after she was married into the family.

'She was working as an interior designer from her MP Nagar office for the past seven-eight years, but I never visited her office. She used to talk a lot on the phone and was very short-tempered. At times, she would start throwing household objects in a fit of anger. I never talked to her, but at times she would try to provoke me to pick a fight. Asad also tried to counsel Zahida on several occasions, but whenever he asked her not to misbehave with us, they ended up fighting. And because of this I stopped telling him about Zahida's behaviour,' Sabiha said.

Among her office staff, no one had anything good to say about her. 'She was short-tempered, unreasonable and would often shout at people without any reason,' was the common observation.

Shakib Danger

Shakib, the eldest son of Hafiz Ali, who is popularly known as Kanpuri Hakeem, never went to school. Police records say he went to school up to class three but no one in his family remembers him ever going to any formal school. As a child, Shakib revelled in watching ram fights. The very sound of the male sheep banging their heads against each other gave him joy. He started betting on ram fights with whatever money he had from a very early age. Shakib married Noor Jehan at an early age and started a tailoring shop along with his wife. He was popular as a ladies' tailor and his very close friends envied him for his success with women and called him a 'ladykiller'. His friends recalled, 'He is fond of beer and after downing a couple of bottles, he would often boast about his women conquests.' Shakib once confided to his friend, 'A very wealthy woman wants to spend a lot of money on me, but her only condition is that I get married to her.' He, however, never revealed the name of this wealthy woman.

While working as a tailor, he met a girl from Idgah Hills whom he befriended and through her got entry into her house. Later, he eloped with this girl, Seema, without bothering to divorce his first wife. He started staying with her at his Nariyal Kheda house in the old city. Shakib sold off his Nariyal Khera house after his mother's death and returned to his first wife. From the money that he got from selling the house, he bought a car and started plying taxis between Indore and Bhopal. He also bought a Tata Indigo car, which he himself used when not ferrying passengers between Indore and Bhopal.

From being a 'ladykiller' he gradually moved into the world of crime. The first case registered against him was at the Nishatpura police station in the year 1990 for trespassing and stabbing. In 1991, three cases for causing hurt, trespassing and issuing life threats were registered against him. This continued till 1992, after which he graduated from a knife-carrying small-time criminal to someone who had an Arms Act case registered against him. He started dabbling in small-time extortion and was always on the lookout for people who could hire his services in order to recover property and debts.

In 1994, a case for attempt to murder was registered against him at the Tallaiya police station. He was declared a habitual offender and for the first time, action under Section 3 of the Madhya Pradesh Public Security Act was taken against him and he was asked to leave Bhopal city.

By the year 2002, Shakib had earned the alias Danger. He was now known as Shakib Danger. There were several cases registered against him, he had already been shunted out from Bhopal and was now out on bail after being arrested for allegedly killing someone under the Khajoori Sarak police station area.

By January 2011, he had a heavy dossier with twenty-eight criminal cases registered against his name. Like any seasoned criminal, he acquired political patronage as well. He got into the inner circles of the ruling party and got himself photographed on stage with the party's state president and its district president. Shakib also obtained a character certificate from a local leader, who described him as a social worker.

Shakib kept his passion for ram fights alive, even as he desperately tried to enhance his stature in the world of crime. And his partner in ram fights was Salim, a hockey player, who had got employment in the Bharat Heavy Electricals Limited under the sports quota. The two together indulged in various other pleasures, apart from betting on ram fights.

Another childhood friend of Shakib was Shadab Khan who managed a gym. Shakib confided a lot in Shadab as he never asked him any questions. Shakib would often borrow Shadab's motorbike and keep it for days together. Such was the friendship between the two that Shadab never asked for his bike back.

The CBI now wanted to move on to working out the association between Zahida Parvez and Shakib Danger, but for this they needed to grill Zahida Parvez. Zahida, until now, had shown no signs of remorse, nor was she anywhere close to giving up. She firmly held on to her initial statement, 'I'm innocent and I'm being framed.'

Before the end of the day, the investigators once again reminded the accused that their game was over. 'The sooner you reveal the entire truth the better it would be for you,' they said as a good night message.

1 March 2012 started on a depressing note for the CBI. Rekha Sangwan missed her flight and she was expected only in the evening now. Separate teams had already been formed to question Zahida and Shakib. A CBI team assisted by the Uttar Pradesh Special Task Force was in Kanpur to question Irfan about whom not much was known. The teams exchanged notes after every round of questioning. Bothra was overseeing the questioning at the CBI office, while Kumar had already set about doing what he knew best: collecting more forensic evidence as no eyewitness was willing to come forward.

At around 2.00 p.m., Bothra called Masood Sultan on his mobile phone and asked him to come over to the CBI office at the earliest. The events of 16 August 2011, the day his daughter was killed minutes after she had said goodbye to him, were playing in Masood Sultan's head. He was breaking down every five minutes and was not in a position to drive. Shehla's cousin Rajil was called and he took Masood Sultan to the CBI office.

Inside the Arera Colony office, Masood Sultan got another shocker. Bothra told him how Zahida had used Shehla's office attendant Irshad to spy on her. As evidence, he showed the father Irshad and Zahida's call details.

Masood Sultan was shocked. Irshad, who seemed to suffer from some hearing impairment had been working with Shehla for the past many years. He knew everything about Shehla's movements and Irshad was the last person she had called on 16 August, before she was shot dead. In his initial statement to the CBI, Irshad had said, 'She asked me to take out her cheque book and the Anna Hazare banner, and wait for her in office.' Irshad knew all about who came to her office, when she was travelling, the places that she travelled to outside the city, what time she came in to office when she was in Bhopal, and the people that she was in regular touch with. He had given a detailed statement, but there was not a word about Zahida.

A few days after the murder, Irshad had come to Masood Sultan's house asking him for his monthly salary. Masood Sultan was worried about his family and promised him that he would take care of him and his family till he got another job.

The previous evening, on 29 February, a day after the alleged masterminds of Shehla's murder were arrested, Irshad was confronted with the mobile phone records that Bothra had just shown to Masood Sultan. The mobile records showed that Irshad was in constant touch with Zahida and now there was no escape for him. And out came the secret behind his conversations with Zahida. Irshad spilled the beans.

On being asked what kind of a person Shehla is, I state that she was a snooty person who had a short temper and thought too much of herself. She was also very greedy.

Shehla's attitude towards me was not good and I was also not paid well. Shankar, who used to clean the office, asked me one day why I was taking the humiliation and why I did not just quit the job. Shankar, too, was not happy with Madam's attitude. Knowing that Shankar worked in many offices, I asked him to look for a job for me.

A few days after this conversation, Shankar told me that he had found a job for me in a nearby office. He asked me to accompany him, but I could not go with him as I was busy. One day, Shehla madam was out and I was just about to leave with Shankar when Madam called me and I could not go.

One day, Shankar told me that the person to whom he had spoken to about me was asking for me. He asked for my number, saying that he would pass it on to her. I gave him my number and after two-three days, a madam called me saying she was Zahida. She gave Shankar's reference and asked me to come over to her office. I told her that I have to stay in the office to attend to the landline phone calls, and she said that I could come over to her office whenever I had the time.

The same day after about an hour, Zahida called me again and asked me why I did not come. I gave her the same reply that I was busy. She kept the phone down and after a little while called up and said, 'I'm sending my boy. Come along with him to my office.'

After some time, a person came to the Miracles office and I went with him to Zahida's office. In her office, she asked me how much salary I received. I told her I was getting Rs 4,000 per month. She said that Shankar had told her that I was loyal to Shehla, but Shehla did not take good care of me. She offered me Rs 5,000 per month, saying that she would take proper care of me. She also said that I could join her office any time I wished. I told her that I would join only after taking my month's salary from Shehla. All this happened sometime around March.

When I did not go to her, she called me again after Holi, almost ten days after our previous conversation and asked me why I had not joined her office. I told her I would not be able to join her and she said, 'My doors are always open for you.'

After another ten days, she called and again asked me why I had not joined her office and then she started asking me about Shehla Masood's location. I told her that she was in Delhi. She asked me about the date of her return and disconnected the phone when I told her that Shehla does not inform me before travelling anywhere.

After some time, she called me again, and this time tried to seduce me so I would tell her about Shehla Masood's movements. She asked me who all came to Shehla's office. She specifically asked if Darbar came to her office or not. I told her that he used to come earlier, but now he did not.

After almost three months, she called me again in July and started by saying that I was more bothered about Shehla than myself. She asked about Shehla and I told her that she was in America and when I said that I did not know when she would be coming back, Zahida disconnected the phone.

In April, a day after Shehla started an indefinite hunger strike supporting Anna Hazare's campaign against corruption, Zahida called me and said, 'Why is she sitting on a hunger strike? Since when has she become a social worker? Does she sit there at night as well or goes home? One who is herself corrupt, what kind of social work will she do?'

> [...]
>
> Five or six days before Shehla's murder, she called me and asked me, 'Are you fasting for Ramzan?' She then asked about Shehla, 'Has she returned from America?' I said yes. Then she asked if Shehla also kept the Ramzan fasts. When I told her that Shehla was fasting, she said, 'Since when has she become so noble? Does she eat when she is alone?'
>
> [...]
>
> On being asked, I further stated that I had once told Shehla that a madam named Zahida asks about her movements, to which she said, 'Let her ask. What can she do?'

Bothra had called Masood Sultan to introduce him to Additional SP AGL Kaul, the new investigating officer on the case. After the formal introduction, the two spoke for over twenty minutes. When Masood Sultan was about to leave, he was asked if he wanted to see the woman who had got his daughter murdered. Sultan trembled, closed his eyes, composed himself again and refused the offer. 'What will I do by seeing her? I have already lost my daughter,' he said.

Shehla's cousin, Rajil, who till now had been silently listening to the conversation, said that he wanted to see both Zahida and Danger. But Kaul politely refused, saying that human beings are the same everywhere. 'It's just that they have lost it in the head. What will you get by seeing them? We will try and ensure that your sister gets justice,' he said.

Just as Masood Sultan and Rajil were stepping out of the CBI office, Bothra's phone rang again. It was around 4.30 p.m. and Kumar was on the line. He sounded excited and said just one line, 'We have nailed her. You please come over.' Bothra immediately started for Design Era, Zahida's first-floor office opposite the Chittod complex in MP Nagar zone 1, which was just a few hundred metres away from Miracles, Shehla's office in Rama Complex.

Immediately after Zahida's arrest on 28 February, CBI officers had sealed Design Era in the presence of two independent witnesses. A seal impression was obtained on the lock and the brass seal was handed over to one of the witnesses. Security guards had also been deployed outside the sealed office.

On 1 March 2012, five cars stopped outside the Chittod complex at around 3.00 p.m. Kumar was in the first car. The second car contained a team of three CBI inspectors, and the third car carried two forensic experts from CFSL, who had come down from Delhi. Two officers from Bharat Heavy Electricals Limited and two officers from Bharat Sanchar Nigam Limited also came in two separate cars. In the fifth car were Asad Parvez and a friend of Zahida Parvez.

All twelve people headed straight to Design Era and at 3.15 p.m. The seal on the lock on the main gate was examined first. It was found to be intact. And the two independent witnesses, who were from the four officers from BHEL and BSNL, identified their signatures, after which the seal was broken and the lock opened. Everything happened in front of Asad Parvez and Zahida's friend, who accompanied him wherever he went.

Kumar stood in one corner. The four officers from BHEL and BSNL stood next to him. Asad Parvez and Zahida's friend also stood in one corner, as the CBI officers and forensic experts started searching. The CFSL experts also shot pictures and a video of the entire search.

Every drawer, every computer, every desk and every wall was searched. From the main hall where Zahida's employees sat, a total of eight items were recovered and seized. These included four computer hard disks, three registers that had recorded entries of people who had visited Design Era between 18 May 2010 and 28 February 2012, and an attendance register that recorded the attendance of the employees between January 2011 and February 2012.

In the wooden shelf behind Zahida's chair, the CBI sleuths saw neatly stacked files. On the top was a file titled D. Inside this file, newspaper cuttings related to Darbar were neatly arranged. There were seventeen cuttings in total and most of them had photographs of Darbar at various public functions. The file was immediately shown to Kumar. Why did Zahida maintain a record of news stories related to Darbar? Kumar was confused. Darbar's name had figured as a possible suspect during the investigations, but what was his connection with Zahida? He could already smell a new angle to the case.

Kumar asked his team to search further and out tumbled another file. It was titled SM. Inside it were newspaper cuttings related to Shehla Masood. Two clippings were from April 2011, when Shehla had sat on a hunger strike supporting Anna Hazare's India Against Corruption campaign. Other clippings were of news items related to the Shehla Masood murder. The clippings followed a pattern. The file maintained a record of all those who were questioned in connection with the murder. A news item related to Savan Bhado's acceptance that he knew Shehla was also preserved.

From the drawer on which a printer was kept, the CBI found four diaries. On the top was one titled Canara Bank; it was the latest, for the year 2012. Right below it was another diary, which had 'Friends Forever' written on it. The CBI officers flipped through the first diary and realized that Zahida had the habit of maintaining a diary. Kumar shouted, 'Look for the 2011 diary!' And there it was, titled AR Electrical. The officer immediately passed on the diary to Kumar, who began flipping through it and looked for an entry dated 16 August. 'She is gone,' he said aloud. The very next moment, he was on the phone, calling up Bothra, 'We have nailed her!'

Bothra reached the Design Era office within ten minutes of receiving the call. Inside the office, Kumar sat on a chair reading the diary. The moment he saw Bothra, he opened the entry dated 16 August and passed it on to him.

Bothra read it aloud. Everyone present in the office listened.

> She is shot dead in front of her house. I was depressed since from the early morning. All of sudden, Ali called up around 11.15 a.m., that, mubarak ho sahib (congratulations), now we did it in front of her house. I was in office. Due to Ramzan, I came early. I sent 'Rohit' also to watch her car. He said car is not parked there. Then I returned back to my home for saying prayers. I became so relaxed, went to Masjid, did prayers. So many calls were missed on my mobile. Regarding only for the information of this incident. Around 12.30 p.m., Sanjay also called but call was missed. Then I called him back. He said this is too much yaar, nafrat ki intehaan hai ye to (This is like extreme hatred), 'darbar' ko Brijesh Lunavat nain inform kiya tha as per Arun statement (Darbar was informed by Brijesh Lunavat as per Arun's statement). Brijesh nain kuch kaan main kaha aur dono uth kar chale gaye (Brijesh said something in his ear and both got up and left).
>
> Hamne shaam main RABAB ka birthday celebrate kiya. Do-do cake kate. Par hum dono ki hi fat rahee thee, raat main Sabah chali gayi, par maine usko phir vapis bulwa liya. Hum log raat bhar jagte rahe. TV dekhte rahe. Aakhon se neend koson durr thi, raat mein Sabah ko Sehri ke liye uthaya to

> ve ekdum chauk gayi (We celebrated RABAB's birthday in the evening. Cut two cakes but both of us were scared. In the evening Sabah left, but I called her back. We were awake the whole night. We watched TV. We could not sleep. I woke Sabah up in the morning for sehri and she got scared).
>
> Phir hum ne sath mein sehri kari – that is all for the day. Sare newspaper, sare channels sub uske murder story se bhare hue the. (We ate for the sehri together – that is all for the day. All the newspapers and news channels were full of her murder story).
>
> Ye natak chala, uske murder ke bees din baad tak (This went on for twenty days after her murder).

Bothra read the diary entry dated 16 August twice and then looked towards Zahida's friend, who was standing next to Asad Parvez. 'Who is Sabah?' he asked. She was the same girl who had wrapped a scarf around her face and given a sound bite to the TV channels outside the women's police station the previous day. She had alleged that her friend was being framed.

Bothra stared into her eyes and she went blank. Her game was up.

Sabah Farooqi had one thing in common with Zahida. She too was not brought up by her parents. She was a little less than two years old when her mother died. Her khala (mother's sister) Anwar Jehan, who herself did not have any children, had adopted Sabah and her elder sister Farah and brought the two girls up at her house in the Shyamla Hills area in Bhopal. Sabah's father, Wahid Farooqi, did not marry again and financially supported his two daughters till he died sometime around 2008. Both sisters went to English-medium school Shishu Vihar and did their post-graduation in commerce from

Maharani Laxmi Bai College in Bhopal. Sabah also did a course in computer science.

Wahid Farooqi owned agricultural land on the outskirts of the city, which Sabah and Farah sold after his death. Sabah started a departmental store 'All Seasons' with her share of the money in the Bagh Mughalia area. She suffered heavy losses in the business and was forced to shut it down. She was desperately looking for a job when her elder sister Farah introduced her to Dr Ayesha. Ayesha knew Farah through her brother Mohamad Naved who owned a security agency 'MP Security and Detective Force'. Naved's agency provided security services at the Narmada Valley Hydroelectric Development Corporation, where Farah worked as a receptionist. Ayesha had two back-to-back operations and she had no one to look after her. It was Sabah who took care of her at that time. Sabah's uncle Sehjad Khan (Anwar Jehan's husband), who had brought up the two sisters like his own children, also thought highly of Sabah's compassion.

Ayesha knew Zahida and she recommended Sabah to her for a job. Zahida kept Sabah in her office and asked her to take care of the accounts. Soon, the two became the best of friends.

According to Anwar Jehan, Sabah was a very good student in school and had no other specific interests. 'She was a quiet girl, who always kept to herself and focused on her studies.'

But now it appeared that Sabah Farooqi was in deep trouble. Bothra started questioning her, while the others resumed their search. They found the diary for the previous two years too: the 2010 one was titled New India Assurance Company Limited, while the one for 2009 was labelled Union Bank.

A few hours into the search and the CBI had already recovered four computer hard disks, one external hard disk, two DVD writers, two laptops, nine mobile phones, twenty-four pen drives, ten SIM cards, twelve memory cards, two digital video cassettes and forty-four CDs from Zahida's cabin. The team, however, had still not reached the drawers of her table.

As the investigators opened the drawers, they realized that they were dealing with sensitive material. They found a used condom packed in an envelope and kept in the side drawer. The same drawer had an envelope inside which a neatly folded paper with 'D hairs' written on it was kept. Inside the folded paper was a lock of hair.

Sabah, by this time, had gone into denial mode and kept on repeating that she did not know anything.

The investigators now realized that it would take a long time for them to get out of the office. The diaries had to be deciphered, the hard disks and other electronic gadgets, including the pen drives had to be scanned, and there was still more evidence popping out of shelves and drawers inside Zahida's cabin. Another file containing thirty pages was found hidden inside one of the table drawers. This file had bank statements, credit card statements, a copy of an FIR she had lodged against one Fazal of her locality, and a duplicate phone bill under Reliance which belonged to Darbar. In between these papers was a handwritten letter addressed to the CBI. The letter was written in Hindi and in the very first line the writer made it clear that a man was writing the letter. The letter read as:

> To
> CBI Bhopal,
>
> I want to bring certain secret facts to your knowledge. Everyone knows that Shehla was misusing her RTI activist status. She was a blackmailer and used to blackmail people against whom she filed applications under the Right to

Information Act. She also had illicit relations with some of these people against whom she had filed the RTI applications. There are several such names, but at the very top is Darbar. Shehla had very close relations with Darbar from 2004 to 2009. This can be confirmed by the CBI from Shehla and Darbar's call details for that period.

The reason why their relationship soured was because she had filed an RTI application against Darbar. Also, she had relations with Savan Bhado. Why did Shehla not leave Darbar even after having a relationship with Savan Bhado?

On what basis was she blackmailing D?

Why had Shehla blocked Darbar's car?

Why has Shehla's husband not come out in front of the media till now?

The CBI was in for yet another surprise. The same file contained the anonymous letter against Shehla in which it was alleged that she was part of a fake currency racket. Shehla was summoned to the police station to give a statement on the basis of this anonymous letter that was addressed to the IG, Shailendra Shrivastava. Shrivastava had referred this complaint to the MP Nagar police station. The CBI had taken this letter into its custody from the MP Nagar police station. How had these two anonymous letters come under Zahida's possession? The CBI was now getting a clearer idea about who was behind maligning Shehla.

The CBI also recovered four other small diaries with various scribbles in them. The scribbles pointed towards Zahida's obsession with Darbar.

By the time the hard disks, CDs and pen drives were scanned and signatures of the witnesses were taken on every seized document, it was already 4.00 a.m. – the search had gone on for more than thirteen hours. At 4.00 a.m., Asad Parvez was handed over a copy of the list of all seized items and documents. Asad Parvez acknowledged the receipt. The office was sealed once again and everyone left MP Nagar. Sabah, however, was not allowed to go home and was taken to the CBI's Arera Colony office instead.

The CBI now had a lot of stuff to confront Zahida Parvez with, but before that could happen, her diaries had to be read. The investigators knew for sure that Zahida's diaries would throw up the real motive for the murder.

Nine

The Sex Diaries

2009

1 January

If you judge people, you have no time to love them – Mother Teresa.

In a day, when you don't come across any problem, you can be sure that you are travelling in a wrong path – Swami Vivekananda.

16 March

I met with Darbar. It was regarding work in the tourism department. He was impressed with me. We hardly spoke for five minutes, and that too through ifs and buts.

I think he really felt something for me. But I didn't feel anything.

17 March

After my meeting with him he tried to talk to me so many times but I refused. I never picked up his call. He felt very bad.

18 March

Simultaneously my affair with Ajeet is going on. I'm talking to him on the phone.

19 March

In the middle of the month [February], somewhere between 23 and 27, I refused to shake hands with him [Darbar]. I refused to sit close to him. In fact, I am afraid to meet him.

3 May

Darbar came to my office for the first time. For the first time, ever since I met him, I felt something for him.

13 May

Somewhere in the first or second week of May, I said yes to Darbar.

I wrote a text message, 'You talk so cheap Darbar but still aap jaise bhi hain, I've started loving you.'

18 May

Darbar fought with me like anything. He abused me. We agreed to finish our relationship.

19 May

We patched up but not in that way. Again he abused me and called me neech kutti kamini.

We decided to finally finish our relationship. I hate him like anything.

20 May

Finally I back off from him. I cried the whole day. I was very disappointed. He wanted to go out for dinner. I refused. I don't want to continue. I hate him. I have finished everything from my side. I have buried all feelings in my heart. I had started loving him but then it is my destiny to be alone. I made myself strong.

My beloved Parvej [Parvez] got bail from court today.

21 May

Nothing can be done in our case. Everything is finished now. I will miss you a lot Darbar.

4 June

Darbar has felt me everywhere. First time I did intercourse with someone other than Parvez.

27 July

Darbar called from the Vidhan Sabha at around 11.00 a.m. 'I thought I should take birthday wishes from you,' he said. I wished, 'Belated Happy Birthday'.

In the evening I left a missed call on Sanjay's number. Darbar called back and asked me why I had called. I asked, 'Do you love me?' He did not say anything.

2010

20 January

Darbar grabbed me. We had sex, but partially. As usual he called me in the afternoon. Asked me for a meeting? I said OK.

He arrived at my office at 7.00 p.m. I was sitting on a chair with my hair open. He saw me and I saw him, we smiled at each other. Immediately he gave me a tight lip touching kiss. I cried a lot and he cajoled me. Then he showed interest in sex. He took off my clothes. We had sex and then he got off.

29 January

Today for the first time I got angry at Ajeet. I took out Darbar's anger on Ajeet. I did not take Darbar's call in the morning. I spoke to Ajeet in front of him but he did not react. I don't know why?

3 February

Initially I decided not to be with him. Darbar sent me a message. I didn't reply. Then he called and asked me to reply via SMS. I did not do that. Then he said OK, 'I will call you again directly and disturb.' He gave a call on the Reliance number but I did not take it...

He finally stopped calling. I really miss him a lot.

There was a power cut in the evening. Power supply was restored at 10.00 p.m. I missed him a lot. I cried for him. Till now he had relations with Shehla M. and S ... simultaneously. This thing is killing me.

15 February

We had sex again. I don't know how many times.

19 February

We had sex inside the cabin at 6.15 p.m. 'Why do you have sex without a condom. Are you not afraid, what if you get pregnant?' he asked 'It does not make any difference to me. I will give birth to a baby,' I replied. He said, 'No.' Then he said, 'Partner, you were not in the mood today. You just wanted to oblige me.' I said why would I do that? 'Because you love me,' he said. I have compromised with Darbar. He goes to a lot of places. He is physically related with so many other women but I cannot help it.

12 March

At last we part ways. Despite the fact, that we didn't want this to happen...

6 April

Darbar came to office at around 7.30 p.m. We had sex. He asked me to accompany him to Delhi on 13 April. I said, 'Get the tickets done.' He did not say anything after that. He was busy with the elections. 'Whenever I come to you there is some work that I'm missing,' he said. I said don't come. Then he kissed me.

21 April

Darbar went to Delhi for some conference and rally. Suddenly at 10.00 a.m. his wife called up and said, 'I want to meet you.' I was very annoyed. Darbar was very good to me today. We had spoken at 7.00 in the morning. Sanjay called back after I called on his number at noon. He told me some anonymous caller had called at their home and told her about our affair. 'V was furious. She was shouting at both of us,' he said

Darbar came back from Delhi around 8.00 p.m.

22 April

There was a big fight over me at Darbar's house today. Before coming to office, Darbar went to Sanjay and explained to him how his wife had created a scene at home. He spoke to me just once today.

23 April

I was missing Darbar. I planned to create a scene in front of him. I bought glycerine and put it in my eyes and called Sanjay. Darbar and Sanjay arrived at 2.15 p.m. He went away all of a sudden and then I abused him. I messaged and abused that bastard. He tried calling me but I switched of the phone. He had gone for a Red Cross function. The bastard got himself clicked with Tiwari. I wish the bastard dies. The son of a dog called me at 1.00 a.m.

28 April

Today that dog Shree had called. I hate him. I got call details of three numbers today. I have decided that I will bump off that dog.

3 May

It is very difficult to pass the days. I remember him like mad. I don't know whether it is possible to live without him or not? He will also not stay happy. God willing, he will remember me at every step. Whosoever makes me cry, I will not let him stay alive. God willing after this period of silence there will be a big blast. One of us will die.

4 May

Breaking News: Today his wife went to the 45 Bungalows house. She searched everything including his laptop. She is after his life.

She went to the office in his absence.

6 May

He asked me to come to Vidya Nagar. Sanjay explained the address to me. We had sex. I was there for only ten minutes.

12 May

Darbar called from the Vidhan Sabha at around 5.30 p.m. 'I will be there at 7.00 p.m.,' he said. I immediately rushed to VLCC for eyebrows and upper lip treatment.

He came to office after a long time today. He literally refused to have sex. He even refused to kiss me. I cried the whole night.

13 May

Dear diary, I'm very tired. Emotionally I'm broken. I cry a lot. I badly need one companion of my choice. Now I don't even talk to Darbar. I had gone to VLCC today. Went to the office of Aneesh at 7.00 p.m. Ajeet has joined region 6 [telecom circle] now. Now we will be able to talk. I don't miss Darbar that much any more.

7 August

We met in the car. On phone, he told me that he was not even on talking terms with Shehla.

27 August

We met and had sex. He called at 1.00 p.m. and fixed for 2.00 p.m. I said let's not do it today. He said, 'No, I have just come to fuck.' He fucked and left in fifteen minutes.

3 November

That bastard called at uround 10.00 a.m. We spoke for hardly twenty-four seconds. I did not speak to Sabah as well. I wish that this bastard gets a heart attack.

He should never get someone whom he likes and some day I wish he is caught red-handed in his car.

21 November

Today Darbar again cheated on me for that bitch SC. He did not come to meet me.

27 November

He called me twice but I did not talk to that bastard. I hate him. I wish god snatches away everything from him. That bastard Sanjay had also called but I said no for today as well as tomorrow.

12 December

We had sex in my full menstrual cycle. I was bleeding like anything but enjoyed.

2011

11 January

Darbar had come to office today. We tried to have sex but his wife called saying there was a power cut at his home. He immediately ran away. Also, it was the fourth day of my menstrual cycle so he did not want to do it.

13 January

I realized that Darbar was running away from sex. This was the first time. It appeared as if he was afraid of me. He was making excuses. He gifted me a perfume. For the first time it so happened that he did not even touch me. I cried a lot after he left.

28 February

We had sex after a long separation of fourteen days.

I told him that I don't want to make love. He said, 'OK.' We sat together and started talking. He asked me why I behaved like a bitch the other day. I asked him what relation he had with SC. He said he did not have any relationship with anyone except me. I told him that she goes with you. He replied, 'Not only her. You catch me with any other girl. I'm ready to lose everything that I have, including my life. I can give this to you in writing. I may abuse you but…' I told him, 'Darbar not just abuse, you can even hit me, but don't do this.' Then we kissed and hugged and had sex… Then he left, leaving behind those beautiful memories.

2 March

For the first time he said, 'Zahida, I'm thankful to you. Because of your vigilance I have stopped talking to girls. I've given up the habit of making friends with girls. Now I don't talk to anyone.'

10 March

We had sex inside the car outside my office near Chittor complex. I met Darbar at around 7.00 p.m. We had an excellent time. He fingered me like anything. We smooched like mad. He told me his future plans. He said he was planning to move to Delhi as a member of parliament.

7 May

Darbar took off my clothes today. He asked for my tongue. We had sex after a long time of separation. He came back to Bhopal by the 11.00 a.m. Jet airways flight. I called up doc [Darbar's friend] to find out if he was going to pick him up. He said he was already on the way. He sounded rude. I said bye.

29 May

We met and had a little bit of sex. We had just started when his phone started ringing. He lost his erection and I got furious. He said sorry but I did not listen and fought. He even scolded the person who had called.

30 May

Insha Allah we will have sex today. Today's going to be a blast. Darbar is excited since morning. He called and started, 'I love you Jaan. Listen I really want to fuck you today. If you don't pick up a fight today, I'll fuck you really hard. OK tell me what time I should come.' I said, '7.30 p.m., but only if you keep your worries and tension outside. Also, you mustn't even look towards the phone.' 'OK, but you also listen to this thing. You just wait for me nude and lying down,' he replied. I said OK and was about to say something when he cut me short and said, 'Yaar, I will get an erection right now. I have to go out and work.'

2 June

I met Darbar in the afternoon today. It was for just two minutes. He had come to collect his papers.

I came back from Jabalpur today. I checked all my phones but there was no missed call from him. Finally, I found one message, 'hold me close to your bosom'. I called him after waiting for his call till 1.30 p.m. He said he will come to see me and finally turned up at 2.00 p.m.

He was very smartly dressed. I think he was going along with doc to meet someone. He does not come to meet me. He never takes me along with himself. I think he will never be able to love me. He is not able to forget Shehla or he must have got someone else?

Goodbye, Darbar. You are a nice man. You are really very innocent. I'm mad about you. Please give me a little space in your heart. Please. How unlucky I am? I gave away everything that I had but still I could not get your love.

4 June

He loves me and I also love him a lot.

9 June

We had sex. He just pounced upon me. He really enjoyed. He stayed for twenty minutes. Did what he wanted and then left. I felt really bad but did not say anything.

21 June

I don't know why he lied to me. He said he was going somewhere but went to Sanjay's office in Vidyanagar.

We chased them but he and Sanjay saw us and started chasing us instead. We enjoyed chasing you, Mr Darbar Singh.

27 July

We did not talk throughout the day today. I had sent Saini to keep a watch on him. In the evening at exact 7.00 p.m. both he and doctor had gone to Shehla's house. I called up Darbar at around 7.45 p.m. and blasted him like anything. I cried a lot. From the other number I called Shehla and spoke to her for thirty seconds.

28 July

Darbar called up early in the morning around 9 a.m. He was trying to give his clarifications. 'I don't have any affair with any one, neither did I have any affair in the past nor do I want to have,' he said. I also went to an astrologer who said the enemy will vanish and Darbar will come back to me.

15 August

I did not speak to Darbar at all. But he spoke with Shehla twice and that too for over half an hour each time. Poor fellow Darbar, he is finished.

16 August

She is shot dead in front of her house. I was very depressed since morning when, all of a sudden, Ali called up around 11.15 a.m. 'Mubarak ho sahib we did it in front of her house,' he said. I was in my office. I had come early due to Ramzan. I sent Rohit to check her car. He confirmed that the car was not parked. I returned home to offer my prayers. I was so relaxed. I went to the mosque and offered prayers. I had many missed calls registered on my phone ... Sanjay also called around 12.30 p.m. but I missed the call. I called him back and he said, 'This is too much. This is height of hatred.' Brajesh informed Darbar. As per Arun he said something in his ear and both left immediately.

We celebrated Rabab's birthday in the evening. We cut two cakes but both of us were very scared. In the evening Sabah went but I called her back. We watched television throughout the night. We were not able to sleep. When I woke Sabah for sehri [the morning meal eaten before sunrise during Ramzan] she got shocked. Both of us did sehri together. That is all for the day. All newspapers and all news channels were filled with her murder story.

This drama continued for twenty days after her murder.

6 September

Today a long time after the assassination, Darbar surprised me. Dot at 3.45 p.m., Sanjay came to office. Darbar was also with him but he was sitting in the car. It was a white Maruti (number XX). Then Sanjay signalled to him.

20 September

Darbar called from Sanjay's number at around 10.00 a.m. We talked for about ten minutes, he spoke very nicely. 'You were very angry that day,' he said. 'Yes I also felt very bad about it. That's why I was calling you yesterday but you did not take my call,' I replied. 'Sanjay will come to your office to see you today. Meet him. You will feel nice. What time would you be available?' he asked. I said 12.30 p.m.

Sanjay first called at noon. He reached office around 12.35 p.m. He was carrying two mobile phones with him. One was for me, one for Darbar. While having coffee, he said, 'Her diary has been found. She had written a lot of stuff about her appointments...'

The diaries were only about Darbar, sex and passion. It was clear that Zahida could do anything for Darbar. She also had a good memory. On several occasions, she had recorded the entries much after they had actually occurred.

The investigators now had a lot of stuff to confront Zahida with. Also, there was a new direction to the investigations now. This time, it was clear.

Ten

The Love Triangle that Never Was

Inspector Rekha Sangwan walked into the Bhopal CBI office at around 8.00 a.m. on 2 March. She had arrived in Bhopal by the evening flight the day before and had been briefed by the top CBI officers in Delhi.

The previous night the investigators had allowed Asad Parvez to talk to his wife and asked him to tell Zahida that she should tell the truth about Darbar's involvement. Asad had seen with his own eyes what the CBI had recovered from Zahida's office. He had also read portions of her diary. He was devastated. He pleaded with Zahida not to spare the man who had ruined his family.

Inspector Sangwan asked Zahida for a specimen of her writing. She refused. Sangwan told Zahida that her game was up and asked her to cooperate with the investigators, but Zahida was not one to budge.

Sangwan immediately called in two bank officials as independent witnesses. She recorded Zahida's refusal to give the specimen of her writing on a piece of paper in front of the two independent witnesses and pushed it before Zahida to sign it. Zahida again refused.

Then, Sangwan asked for Zahida's diary and called a sub-inspector to read aloud the entry dated 16 August 2011.

The SI hurriedly flipped through the pages and looked into Zahida's eyes as he started reading, 'She is shot dead in front of her house. I was very depressed since from the early morning. All of a sudden Ali called around 11.15 a.m. saying Mubarak ho sahib...'

The SI was reading slowly, pausing after each word. Just then, Zahida started howling, 'It is not me! It is not me!'

'If it is not you, why are you not giving a specimen of your writing?' Sangwan asked. Zahida refused again and the SI was asked to continue reading.

The relevant portions of her diary were read out loud to Zahida. The investigators read out the sexual escapades recorded in the diary as well. They thought Zahida would break down and reveal how the murder had been planned and executed. They were wrong; she refused to accept anything.

Sabah Farooqui, meanwhile, was getting anxious. She was asked to wait in a room. A couple of hours had passed. When an investigator entered the room, Sabah rose to her feet and asked, 'When will I be allowed to go?'

'You will go to jail. But before the court sends you to jail we would like to keep you as our guest. You are under arrest for planning and executing Shehla Masood's murder,' she was told.

Sabah knew what was coming. She was now taken to the room where Zahida was being interrogated. The two embraced each other and started cursing God. Sangwan interrupted their meeting, 'Enough of your drama, now back to business.'

The arrest documents were ready and Sabah was asked to sign them. She signed without much fuss and the inspector recorded the time and place of her arrest: At 12.45 hours on 2 March at the Bhopal CBI office.

Sabah tried to console Zahida. 'Appi, you don't worry. This will pass. We are with these people only for fourteen days. After that they will have to send us to jail. We will apply for bail and we will be free once again,' she said, as she was taken out of the room.

Sabah was the first to crack. Within half an hour, she was ready to sign another memorandum, this time under Section 27 of the Evidence Act.

The investigators had put on paper what Sabah had just told them: 'On 29 February 2012 at about 5.30 a.m. I removed one red-coloured Bajaj discover DTSI Motorcycle, kept hidden inside the store room located at the ground floor of the house of my friend Zahida Parvez located at old Sofia College Road and left this motorcycle near Raja ji ka kuan, Kabristan, Sofia College Road, near the shop of Javed electrician. I'm willing to show the place where I had left the motorcycle.'

Two independent witnesses signed the document alongside Sabah.

The motorcycle belonged to one Abdul Razak and Zahida had taken it away from him when he had come to ask for Rs 40,000, which Zahida owed him. Zahida was doing the interiors of a bakery on Kolar Road in Bhopal and had outsourced some part of the work to him. The motorcycle was used by the gang to follow Darbar.

The investigators now had a clear idea that Darbar was the cause behind the murder. But how was he involved? There was still no direct evidence against him.

The CBI now called it a love triangle. Zahida and Darbar were having an affair. Zahida suspected Darbar was involved with other women including Shehla. She was obsessed with Darbar to such an extent that she was spying on him and had prepared a list of women he met. Zahida and Sabah had also surveyed the house of another girl, Shivani, who they suspected was also involved with Darbar. Sabah had even gone to meet Shivani at her house on the pretext of doing a survey. Sabah had also shown Shivani's house to Shakib.

Zahida suspected that Darbar was ignoring her because of Shehla, hence she decided to eliminate her.

The question that bothered the CBI was the news point in the media. What was Darbar's role in the murder? Zahida, in between throwing tantrums, had accepted that she loved Darbar and was mad about him.

'Did he also love you?' the investigators asked. Her reply was yes.

'Then what was the need to kill Shehla?' Zahida repeatedly went into denial mode at this question.

The CDs recovered from Zahida's office were also being scanned. It was time-consuming, but somewhere around 6.00 p.m., an officer walked into the Bhopal CBI office. He could not say what he had just seen in the CD. Bothra went into the room where the CDs were being scanned and he was shocked at what he saw.

The search party had searched everything and everywhere, but had not checked the walls of Zahida's office.

The CBI had its job cut out for the next day. It was a crucial day – Sabah was to be presented before the special CBI court in Indore on 3 March, and Darbar was to be summoned to the CBI office in Bhopal.

Since early morning, television crews were stationed outside the CBI office and the two government houses allotted to

Darbar. 'It's a matter of time now. In principle, the CBI has decided to arrest Darbar,' the gossipmongers talked amongst themselves. No one, however, had any idea about the evidence against him.

After photographs of Shakib Danger surfaced with senior political leaders, including the state president of a national party, the suspicion was that Darbar had used Zahida to eliminate Shehla through Shakib.

Ever since Zahida's arrest, the speculation in the media was that Darbar would be called in for questioning. He was the central character in the entire story and there was no way he could escape questioning.

Darbar anxiously waited for the call from the CBI, which finally came at around 5.00 p.m. on 3 March. The CBI was now well-prepared to carry out their questioning with Darbar.

The investigations were once again moving forward. The various teams questioning Zahida, Sabah and Shakib were exchanging notes every half an hour.

Shakib told the investigators that Zahida had come in a black Indica Vista car to deliver the money to him once it was confirmed that Shehla was dead. Zahida denied this, saying that she did not own any black car. Shakib insisted it was a black car. People working in Zahida's Design Era office were called to ask if Zahida had ever owned a black car. They confirmed that she had a black car.

Finally, she told the investigators that she had sold the car to Mechman Motors. The company's chief executive officer, Madho Bagree, was questioned. Bagree told the CBI that Zahida called Mechman Motors on 10 February 2012 and enquired about the procedure for purchasing a new car in lieu of an exchange of her old car, which had also been purchased from the same company. Zahida was handed over a new grey-coloured Vista

LX car. That very day she surrendered her old car, which was in her husband Asad Parvez's name. The CBI seized the black car from Mechman Motors.

Sabah was presented before the Special CBI court in Indore at around noon. Her custody for the next three days was secured. Sabah was back in Bhopal by 6.00 p.m. and immediately along with independent witnesses she was once again taken to Zahida's office. She pointed towards the hidden camera that the CBI had missed during their previous search. She also led them to five more CDs that had been carefully hidden inside a box.

Darbar's interrogation started at 3.00 p.m. He accepted that he had a relationship with Zahida, but maintained that he had nothing to do with the murder and that he never thought that Zahida could do any such thing. He also denied knowing Shakib Danger.

At 6.00 p.m., when his investigators took a tea break, Darbar thought that his grilling for the day was over. He sought permission to leave, but an officer told him there was something he should see; something the CBI had found while searching Zahida's office.

He was ushered into a room where four people were already seated. Darbar had not seen any of these four men earlier. A giant projector screen had already been put in place. Darbar sat down on a stool that was offered to him. Behind him sat the four men.

Darbar could not believe what he was seeing. Zahida had secretly recorded all their sexual escapades. Darbar was deeply embarrassed to see himself in flagrante delicto with Zahida, but there was nothing he could do. The four people behind him clapped every four-five minutes, as if applauding his performance. Darbar requested for the movie to be stopped, but the plea was ignored. Unknown to him, the four had been given orders to ensure he saw the entire film. The video lasted for over an hour. Zahida had recorded many of her sexual escapades and there was over four hours of footage.

At the end of the hour, Darbar was barely able to get up. He was taken back to the room where he was previously questioned. The investigators were waiting for him.

He was once again questioned at length and this time he had a great many things to say about Zahida. He pleaded before the CBI officers not to make the footage public. 'I will be finished,' he said. The CBI assured him that his sexcapades would not be leaked, but there was a rider: he would have to cooperate with the investigators. Darbar Singh, notoriously famous for holding his own feudal court, where women and Dalits were not allowed to raise their head, stood before the CBI officers with his eyes boring into his toes. He requested the investigators to allow him to leave using the back door. He could not imagine facing the hungry media waiting outside. He called up an associate and asked him to bring a scooter to the gate at the back of the CBI office, and at around 11.00 p.m. Darbar silently slipped away.

The entire interrogation was secretly recorded. Darbar had blabbered a lot, but what interested the CBI officers the most was his opinion about Zahida. He had used the choicest adjectives.

On Sunday, 4 March, Zahida was shown the video recording of Darbar's interrogation. She now knew what Darbar thought of her. She broke down instantly. She was shattered. For the first time she pointed a finger towards Darbar. She said the money that she had handed over to Shakib was given to her by Darbar. She stated that Darbar was the mastermind behind the murder. The investigators wanted evidence. She pointed towards the fact that on 16 August, Darbar's wife had made two calls, the first to the landline number at Shehla's house and the second to Savan Bhado's office number in Delhi. 'Why was she calling them on the day of the murder?' she asked.

Darbar's wife had already been questioned by the CBI about her mobile phone call details on 25 October 2011. She had no other option but to accept that she had indeed made the two calls. While trying to explain why she had called, she had said in her statement:

> I have been informed that on 16 August around 10.46 a.m. a call of about thirty-one seconds from my mobile phone had been made on the landline phone installed at the residence of Shehla Masood. Another call of about eight seconds was made on the office number of Savan Bhado. I accept that these calls were made by me because my husband was not talking to me properly for the last three-four days. I got suspicious on whether he had again started going around with Shehla. Hence, I thought I should talk to her father and at the last moment it came to my mind that it would not be proper, and hence I asked him if the caller identification facility was available on his phone. Mr Masood said no, and I asked him if he wanted to install the same on his phone. He asked for the tariff and after that, I disconnected the phone.
>
> After that it came to my mind that I should tell the wife of Savan Bhado that her husband was going around with Shehla. I called on the landline, but a male person responded and I disconnected the phone.

What she could not explain was why she did not immediately disconnect the phone, when at the last moment she had decided not to talk to Shehla's father, and why she did not ask for Savan Bhado's wife when a man had picked up the phone in Delhi.

It was at this stage that two opinions surfaced within the CBI about Darbar's culpability. A section within the top CBI leadership felt that Darbar was involved and that Zahida's accusations against him were sufficient. Another section felt that Zahida could not be trusted with her statement. Her diaries had already revealed the state of her mental well-being.

Darbar's opponents within his own party had started alleging that he had 'managed' the CBI through a senior politician of the opposition party, who belonged to the same caste as Darbar. To substantiate their suspicion, they gave the example of how every Thakur politician in UP had united behind Raja Bhaiya when Mayawati as the chief minister had taken action against him. Darbar's enemies had already started looking for evidence against him through state agencies. The CBI officially maintained that no one would be spared if there was evidence.

It was presumed by everybody that Darbar had planted Shakib with Zahida, and through her, had got him to get killers from Kanpur to eliminate Shehla. By doing so he had killed two birds with one stone – got rid of Shehla, as he did not like the fact that she had left him and was in a relationship with Savan Bhado, and relieving himself of Zahida by involving her in the crime since she was pestering him. By doing so, he had created three layers and ensured that there was no evidence against him. Big Boss, who had played a role in taking the case right up to the Union home minister, also believed that there was meat in this theory.

The CBI now needed to unearth how Shakib Danger came into contact with Zahida. Both Zahida and Shakib were being separately questioned on this, but there was a small break in between.

CBI Director AP Singh and Special Director Salim Ali decided to come to Bhopal on 5 March. Every news channel crew was there to receive them at the airport. Singh refused to talk to the media, but he promised that he would do so later.

From the airport he headed straight to the Police Officers' Mess where the entire investigation team was there to meet him.

It turned out that Singh had come to pat the backs of the officers who had worked on the Shehla Masood murder case. Police officers who were deputed from the state police to assist the CBI got awards from the director. He interacted with the media over tea the next morning. Ali explained to the media how the agency had worked through over nine lakh telephone calls and how the killers had been nabbed. However, there were many dots yet to be connected, and the weapon of offence was yet to be recovered.

The immediate task at hand, however, was to find out how Shakib had met Zahida. Who introduced the two? Was it Darbar or someone else on his behalf?

Coincidentally, Zahida and Shakib both mentioned a name in their interrogation: Fazal. Taking a cue from this, the CBI searched for Fazal, but was in for a rude shock. Fazal was already dead. Fazal had committed suicide by consuming poison on 16 October 2011. In his dying declaration to the police, he alleged that he had taken the extreme step because of the depression that resulted from cases that Zahida and Asad Parvez had filed against him at the Shahjahanabad and MP Nagar police stations respectively.

Fazal, around twenty-five years of age, had been working as a recovery agent for Kochhar Plyboards. His main job was to recover money from defaulters. He lived in Zahida's neighbourhood and according to his friends he was once a very good friend of hers. He had got some old houses vacated for Zahida from the tenants of Sajjad Hussain Trust in the Bhopal Talkies area. Zahida wanted to construct new flats after demolishing the old properties. According to Fazal's father,

Hussain, his son managed all the No Objection Certificates (NOCs) for her and for this she owed him six lakh rupees. 'She paid him two lakh rupees, but refused to pay the remaining four lakh rupees. When my son asked for the remaining money, she refused and instead got cases registered against him,' he said.

The first case against Fazal was registered on 7 October 2009 and the complainant was Zahida's husband, Asad Parvez, who alleged that Fazal and his father had attacked him without any provocation.

On 22 January 2010, Asad registered another case against Fazal for threatening to kill him.

The third case against him was registered by Zahida on 2 June 2010, alleging that he had tried to outrage her modesty at her Old Sophia College Road residence.

Fazal was arrested in all the three cases, but in the last case he was sent to jail where he stayed for forty days. In jail, Fazal made friends with Arman, who was serving a sentence for dealing drugs. When the two were released, Fazal went to meet Arman at his house, where he met Shakib. Shakib, who had by that time made a name in settling property disputes, was always on the lookout for recovery related cases. So when Fazal told him that he had to recover money from Zahida, he readily agreed to take over the case.

Shakib met Zahida for the first time in connection with Fazal's money, but was charmed by her and instead offered his services to her. Zahida entrusted him with the task of settling scores with Razak, a mason, who had lodged a complaint against Zahida in the MP Nagar police station for not paying him the money for the work that he had executed for her in one of her projects. In order to show his skills, Shakib snatched Razak's motorbike and handed it over to Zahida. Realizing that Zahida had roped in criminals, Razak gave up the claim over his money as well as his bike.

Shakib thought Zahida was a prize catch and whenever Fazal asked him about what was happening about the recovery of his money, he would raise his palm in a gesture that suggested that things were moving. 'Fazal did not have the guts to ask Shakib a second question,' said Tahir Khan, a school bus driver who met Shakib at his house every day over drinks.

Shakib had told one of his friends about a very rich woman who was after him and wanted to marry him. Zahida also started exchanging messages with Shakib, which gave him ideas. All the while Shakib was falling into her trap, he thought that it was he who was trapping a big fish like Zahida.

Everyone in Fazal's family and among Shakib's friends confirmed that it was because of Fazal that Shakib had met Zahida, and instead of recovering the money from her, he had fallen for her.

The weapon of offence had still not been recovered. Shakib maintained that Shanoo Olanga had taken it to Kanpur. The CBI had no other choice but to believe him. Shakib was having a ball at the CBI office. His handler had assured him that he would be made an approver and that it was just a matter of time before he would be out of the case.

Irfan alias Shyam, who was lodged in the Kanpur Central Jail in connection with an attempt to murder case, was presented before the CBI court in Indore on 9 March. He was now arrested for Shehla's murder and remanded to CBI custody till 16 March.

The third among seven children, Irfan loved the company of criminals and at a very young age met Eidu, who was always on the lookout for fresh faces who could help him in his smack business. Irfan started selling smack for Eidu and earned a daily allowance in return. He was caught on a couple of occasions and sent to jail. Eidu took care of his expenses when he was in jail and also arranged for an advocate who fought his cases. Irfan himself did not consume smack and was into smoking hash. While smoking hash, he realized that selling it was a lucrative business. He bought hash from his contacts, who got it from Nepal, and sold it along with smack in Kanpur.

Irfan had an affair with a widow and mother of two, who lived in his neighbourhood. When he expressed his desire to marry the widow, his father turned him away from his house. He started living separately in a rented house in Begumganj and visited his parents' house occasionally.

Irfan was close to his sisters, who used to call him Shyam Bhai. He was forced to flee Kanpur after he and his friends accidentally shot a UP STF man. Irfan and his friend were selling smack in Kanpur when they were caught by the UP STF team. While they were being searched, Irfan accidentally pulled the trigger of his gun and shot a UP STF constable in the foot. Babloo, a fellow inmate had helped him to get out of Kanpur. Once the matter with the UP STF was settled, Irfan returned to Kanpur and resumed his work. This was the first attempt to murder case registered against him.

On 9 March, the day Irfan was arrested in connection with the Shehla Masood murder, the CBI moved an application in court seeking to record Darbar's willingness to undergo a polygraph test. Darbar had already committed his willingness to undergo the test to the CBI and a formal consent was given by his lawyer in court. Darbar was asked to report at the CBI head office in Delhi on 14 March.

All suspects, Irfan, Shakib, Zahida and Sabah were now being questioned simultaneously.

The search for the fifth man, Salim was still on. The only description that Irfan gave was his height and hair colour.

The CBI and the Uttar Pradesh Special Task Force were now searching for a middle-aged Salim who had a bulging tummy and red hair. The dossiers of all D2 Gang members were scanned. No one fit this description.

In Bhopal, the CBI questioned Tahir Khan and other friends of Shakib. They knew of only one Salim, who worked at BHEL and was friends with Shakib. This Salim was also a ram fight enthusiast like Shakib and Tahir.

Zahida and Shakib completed fourteen days in CBI custody on 13 March. The same day they were presented before the court along with Sabah. The CBI had already taken a written consent from all three for their willingness to get their statements recorded before the magistrate under Section 164 of the Criminal Procedure Code. This statement, the CBI thought, would seal the case. The CBI did not seek any further custody of the three accused, as it moved the application for recording their statements under Section 164. All three were remanded to judicial custody and were sent to the jail at Indore.

The next day, on 14 March Zahida was to get her statement recorded before the magistrate under Section 164. On the same day, Darbar's polygraph test was to be conducted in Delhi.

Zahida reached the court at 11.00 a.m. Everyone except the court reader was asked to leave the courtroom. There were just three people inside the court: the presiding magistrate Dr Shubra Singh, Zahida Parvez and the court reader, ready to take the statement.

Before Zahida was administered the oath, Dr Shubra Singh asked the reader to note:

> I, Dr Shubra Singh, Special Judicial Magistrate CBI and Economic Offences Indore, have told Zahida Parvez, wife

> of Asad Parvez that she is not bound by the court to make any confessional statement and that if any such confessional statement is made by her, it can be used as evidence against her. I'm confident that after explaining this to her, it is her own desire to get her statement recorded.

At the same time, Darbar had also reached the CBI office in Delhi. He was aware that Zahida was getting her statement recorded under Section 164 in Indore. During her previous interactions with journalists outside the Indore court Zahida had already pointed an accusing finger towards him. What if she implicated him in her confessional statement? The polygraph expert was ready with his questions, but Darbar was extremely anxious. He was asked to relax.

In Indore, the court reader started typing, as Zahida began her statement.

1) My name is Zahida Parvez. I'm an architect by profession. I completed my studies in the year 2000 from Mumbai. I was born in Jabalpur on 17 December 1975. My mother handed me over to my maternal uncle and aunt when I was just three years old. I call my maternal uncle as Abba (father) and my aunt as Ammi (mother). My parents had already divorced when I was born. I was born at my maternal grandparent's house. After some time, my mother again started staying with my father, but my maternal uncle and aunt kept me with themselves. I have two real brothers. One is in Ujjain, while the other is in Gadarwara. I also have one sister who stays with her husband in Nagpur.
2) My maternal uncle has always treated me like his own daughter, but my aunt could never accept me.

3) In 1996, I got married to Asad Parvez of Bhopal from whom I have two daughters. My elder daughter is eleven years old, while my younger daughter is six years old. During this time, I completed my post-graduation. In 2004, I opened my office and started work as an architect and interior designing consultant. I made good progress in work. I was busy with my life while my husband was busy with his life. During this time, I contacted the Madhya Pradesh tourism department. At that time Darbar was the chairman of the MP tourism department. I had met Darbar at his 45 Bungalows office in March 2009. I gave my profile to him and he assured that I would get empanelled with the department. He also assured that he would help in getting work for me. He was impressed by me during our first meeting itself. He had my phone number. Gradually he started contacting me. He asked me out for coffee and I went along with my friend. He objected to this saying I should have come alone. Gradually we started talking more and our friendship grew stronger.
4) By April 2009, our friendship had further strengthened and he had already started liking me. Around that time, I responded to his advances and our relationship grew more intimate. Both of us knew that the other was married.
5) When our relationship became intimate, I knew this thing that Darbar had a relation with a woman named Shehla Masood. I had discussed this thing with him but he told me that his relationship with Shehla had ended. And since I loved him I believed in whatever he told me. Gradually I came to know that he had relationships with other women as well. I used to confront him on this but he always denied. We used to meet once or twice a week.

6) In 2009–10, Shehla Masood went to Delhi. I never met her nor did I ever speak to her on the phone. I knew just this thing about Shehla Masood that she was the girl friend of Darbar and that she used to run an event agency called Miracles. After coming to know that Darbar had relations with other women, I used to get him followed by my men and he knew about this. He himself also used to follow me to check if I'm following him or not.
7) In August–September 2010, a man identifying himself as Abbas called me on the phone. When he called me for the first time he said he had some land and that he wanted to plot it. I told him that I would get back to him but I never did. After three-four days he called again and said he was a contractor and talked about the same land. I asked him to come over to my office with the land papers but he came without papers. From his looks, he did not appear to be a decent man. The buttons of his shirt were open and he was wearing karas (bangles) on his hands. He met me twice but he did not get the papers. During his second meeting, he said he was also into getting houses vacated and recovering money. At that time, I was working for Dev Bakery. One mason had run away with my money. I asked Abbas to recover my Rs 30,000 from this mason. Abbas got both Abdul Razak and his motorcycle to my office. In front of Abbas it was decided that Abdul Razak would take his motorcycle after returning my Rs 30,000 to me. When he did not return the money for a long time, my friend Sabah got the colour of this motorcycle changed from black to red from some mechanic in Kilol Park. That bike was just parked at home.
8) Around the same time I got to know that Darbar was also having relations with a woman named Shivani. I got him

chased by my employees. Darbar and Shivani were caught together, but my men could not record a video nor could they click any picture. Since Abbas was in my contact, Sabah showed him Shivani's house and we asked him to chase her and inform us about the places she went to and the people that she met. I also asked him to take photographs and make videos. He asked me, 'Why this woman has to be chased?' I told him, 'She is having an affair with my husband.' Abbas never gave me any information about her. He just said, 'She does not move out of her house.'

9) 26 July 2011 was Darbar's birthday. I got a cake in my office and celebrated his birthday. I spoke to him on 27 July and asked him to come in the evening. He refused, and I got suspicious. I asked my man to chase him, and from him I came to know that Darbar along with his friend Dr Aggarwal had gone to Shehla's house. My man told me that Dr Aggarwal waited in the car while Darbar went to meet Shehla. It was around 7.00 p.m. At around 7.45 p.m. Darbar left Shehla's house. I called him from a land line [sic] phone and asked him, 'Why had you gone to meet Shehla when you have told me you have nothing to do with her?' We had a fight over this and he said, 'I have met Shehla two times before this. This is the first time that you came to know about it.' 'I will tell Shehla everything about our relationship. You cannot do this. You will have to choose one of us,' I threatened him. Darbar did not say anything on this. In the meantime, I called up Shehla on her regular phone from my mobile phone. For thirty seconds she kept on saying hello hello… but I did not have the courage to say anything to her. This was my first and last call to her.

10) On 28 July 2011 I got a call from a private number on my Docomo number which starts with 810 and ends with 706.

> It was Darbar. It was around 8.30 a.m. He started giving his clarifications saying he loved me. 'I'm not meeting her. She keeps calling me on the phone asking me to come. I have got fed up. You are there, she is there, and then there is my wife. You three have turned me mad,' he said. DIG CBI told me that the real name of Abbas is Shakib Danger. I did not know this. I believed in whatever he told me about himself. I have not killed anyone, nor have I conspired to kill anyone. I don't know the reality of Shakib Danger, nor do I know how he executed this murder. I have no idea about the vehicle that he used and the people through whom he got the murder executed. I don't know any Irfan, nor do I know any shooter. I have never spoken to them nor have I ever met them. And even today if Irfan is made to stand before me I will not be able to recognize him. I have not given any vehicle, as is being said by CBI and Shakib Danger.
>
> I don't have anything more to say.

At the end of her statement, Judge Singh once again noted that before Zahida made the statement, she was told that she was not bound to give the above-mentioned confession, and that if she made a confession, it could be used as evidence against her.

The statement was read out to Zahida and she accepted that whatever was written was correct and narrated by her.

In Delhi, Darbar was asked a couple of questions, but his heartbeat refused to normalize. Ultimately, the polygraph test had to be given up. Darbar returned to Bhopal. He knew the next call from the CBI could come any time.

Irfan, who was formally brought into CBI custody on 9 March 2012, repeated the story that Shakib had narrated.

On 15 March, Irfan got cornered for the first time after a constable in the Bhopal police tipped off a top CBI officer that the Shanoo Olanga story being floated was fake.

For this, Naresh Korde, who was the best in the business of making sketches, was brought to town. Irfan was questioned about his stay in Bhopal and the name of Babloo Chonga came up after much persuasion.

A team went to search for Chonga in the area where Irfan said he had stayed. He refused to give a specific location and the team found no one by the name of Chonga in the area. Head constable Nigam's help was sought, since he was the one who had tipped them off, and soon it was clear that Irfan was referring to Babloo Chauka as Babloo Chonga.

Korde had also drawn a sketch based on the description given by Irfan, and a team was sent to get Chauka. His house was locked. Neighbours informed them that they had not seen him for over a month. Nigam now got hold of a relative of Shakib, who was also a friend of Babloo. A deal was struck. Babloo, who was staying in Kanpur at that time, said that he was willing to be questioned in Bhopal.

Babloo arrived at the CBI office in Bhopal on 15 March. He was first shown his own sketch that Korde had made on the description given by Irfan, and was shocked by its accuracy.

Babloo started with his history and how he came to Bhopal.

Babloo was first known as Babloo Lamba (tall). At Anwarganj, his locality in Kanpur, the only distinction was his height. At six feet two inches, he was the tallest among the suppliers of hash and countrymade guns. Babloo himself did not know how he came to be called Babloo Chaura (wide).

He had several cases pending against him in Kanpur and after his marriage, his wife coaxed him into leaving the illegal gun supply trade. He shifted to Bhopal and started selling shoes and slippers. He got shoes and slippers at a wholesale price from Kanpur and retailed them in Bhopal and surrounding areas. The business helped him survive, but soon he was back in the business of supplying hash and illegally made guns. Now he got hash from Nepal and countrymade guns from Kanpur and sold them in Bhopal and around.

Babloo became a contact for those who came from Kanpur to sell hash and guns. Most of the dealers would come to him and he knew about everyone's activities. Many of his visitors were first-time criminals, who would commit crimes for money in Madhya Pradesh and escape to Kanpur. Babloo soon became a sought-after man in police circles for the information he had on the movement of those indulging in criminal activities.

He gave up the gun trade and now just dealt in hash and Kanpur-made shoes and slippers, as many in the police department started cultivating him as a source. It was a mutual agreement: he would provide information on the movement of criminals and the police agreed to turn a blind eye to his hash business.

In Bhopal, Babloo used to play cricket whenever he and his friends got the time. Once while playing at Nariyal Khera, he hit four consecutive fours and he got the name Chauka (four). From that day onwards everybody started calling him Babloo Chauka. In his locality, the easiest way to trace him was through the alias Chauka.

Amongst his regular visitors from Kanpur was Irfan alias Shyam. He had first met Irfan when he was serving his term at the jail at Kanpur. He himself had been undergoing trial under the Arms Act, while Irfan had been undergoing trial under the NDPS (Narcotics Drugs and Psychotropic Substances) Act. He had been caught selling smack for his boss, Eidu.

After getting out on bail, Babloo got Irfan to Bhopal and introduced him to the shoe trade. Irfan had a nasal voice and could never pronounce 'Chauka' correctly. Maybe that's why Chauka's name was heard as Chonga when Irfan uttered it. Irfan had initially stayed with Babloo for a while, but when things cooled down in Kanpur, he returned and started working for Eidu once again.

The CBI made Babloo meet Irfan. Both accepted that they knew each other well. 'Why didn't you tell me that you were about to do such a big thing? Had you told me, I would not have let you do such a thing,' Babloo told Irfan, as he admitted before the CBI that Irfan had stayed at his house in August 2011.

'He came to me in the first week of August and stayed with me for several days. He initially did not disclose anything about the purpose of his visit, but when I insisted he said that Shakib had to settle a property dispute and to intimidate was required to fire a shot in the open.' Irfan nodded as Babloo narrated his story.

'Irfan again came to my house somewhere in the second week of August. During his second visit, he had just stepped into my room when he got a call and said that he had to go as Shakib was calling him. Out of curiosity, I walked some distance with Irfan and noticed that Shakib was carrying a polythene bag in which there were some clothes. At some distance, I saw Tabish. Irfan tried to signal to him to move out of the way, but I could see that he was there in front of the house of Kashmiri alias Riaz, a cousin of Shakib.

'On the day of the crime Irfan left my room at around eight in the morning. He came back around 4.00 p.m. in the evening. I was not at home, but my wife who was washing clothes at that time, said that he had asked her to wash his shirt and when she refused, he put it inside a polythene bag and left wearing one of my shirts. He also took Rs 100 from my wife.'

The CBI now showed Babloo the second sketch Korde had made according to Irfan's description. The CBI investigators were shocked by what came next. Babloo looked at the picture and pointed out that the man whom Irfan had described and was referring to as Salim was, in fact, Babloo's neighbour in Kanpur, who was a driver and had nothing to do with Irfan.

At this point, Irfan confessed that no one named Salim had participated in the crime. 'It was Tabish who was with us that day and I did not name him because Shakib asked me not to.'

Shakib was already in judicial custody and the CBI could not question him.

Irfan was now asked to give the exact details about Tabish and to explain his role in the crime. The investigators soon realized that Shakib had taken them for a ride. Babloo also confirmed that Shanoo Olanga had not come to Bhopal.

'But how can you be so sure that Shanoo Olanga had not come to Bhopal?' he was asked.

'Firstly, he had set up his extortion racket in Kanpur and leather merchants went to his house and gave him several lakhs as protection money every week. He would certainly not come to Bhopal for a few lakh rupees. And even if he had come, he would have certainly come to me or to Fiaz, his best friend.'

By this time, Shanoo Olanga's history had been collected and the CBI realized that Babloo was not bluffing. Shanoo had run an extortion racket in Kanpur. He had been a part of the D2 Gang. But the CBI did not want to take any chances.

Babloo took the investigators to Fiaz's house. He and his brother had gone to sell utensils in an urs (religious gathering) in Rajgarh. A team was immediately dispatched. Fiaz and his brother were picked up in the middle of the night and brought to Bhopal. In Bhopal, Fiaz accepted that Shanoo Olanga had visited him in the past, but that was some three years back.

The CBI was now sure that both Shakib and Irfan had been bluffing all this while. Babloo, too, coaxed Irfan to tell the real story. He also told the investigators that Irfan did not know how to ride a motorcycle.

Irfan realized his game was up and he had no other option but to tell the truth. 'Shanoo Olanga had never come to Bhopal. This story was cooked up by Shakib, who had come to Kanpur along with Tabish in the third week of February, about ten days before I was arrested. Shakib told me that the CBI was zeroing down on us and had started questioning people close to him and that he would soon have to give a statement. He asked me to tell this story and in return promised me that money would be regularly sent to my wife. He asked me to accept the crime and say that the trigger was pulled by Shanoo Olanga and by doing so, he said, both of us would escape criminal liability and within a few months both of us would be out.'

The CBI knew that the rest of the story would have to be corroborated by Tabish. Korde was ready with his sketch; both Babloo and Irfan agreed that it was an accurate image of Tabish.

Just to make sure of things, Nigam was once again brought in to look at the picture created of Tabish. Nigam's source had also confirmed that Tabish was at his house in Kanpur. No one in the UP STF had seen Tabish. Babloo was taken along to Kanpur to help the CBI and the UP STF team identify Tabish.

In Kanpur, a joint team of the CBI and UP STF met Babloo near the Som Dutt Plaza in Navin Market. Babloo went to Tabish's locality and found him strolling outside his house. The two greeted each other, Babloo rolled a joint and during the conversation Babloo asked for Tabish's phone number. 'Brother, I have come from Bhopal to buy .32-bore cartridges.

If you can help me, I can come to you again tomorrow. You take my number and give me a call when you have arranged the cartridges.' Tabish agreed and the two exchanged their numbers before bidding each other goodbye.

Outside the locality, Babloo gave the number to the CBI-STF team, saying that Tabish could be called on the number and subsequently picked up.

But the team was wary about going in. They did not want to go in the Begumganj area as they feared the chances of a riot breaking out. The best way was for Babloo to call Tabish out on some pretext.

Babloo called up Nigam for advice, who also requested him to help out the team. Babloo then called Tabish on his mobile. 'Brother, I'm standing at the cycle market behind your locality. I want to buy a tricycle for my son. If you can come and stand here they will give me some discount. Also, we will discuss the price of the cartridges.'

Tabish fell into the trap and was at the cycle shop within ten minutes. It was a Sunday and there were not many people in the otherwise crowded market. In the intervening ten minutes, Babloo had already rolled two joints. They stepped into an isolated corner to smoke the joints and had just finished one, when the CBI-STF team started closing in from all sides. Tabish's game was up. Both Babloo and Tabish were bundled into a waiting jeep and a mask was immediately put around Tabish's head.

The CBI team in Bhopal was immediately informed with the message: 'Operation successful'. A two-member team was immediately rushed to Kanpur to formally arrest Tabish and bring him to Bhopal. The team reached Kanpur on 19 March. Tabish was arrested and was first taken to Lucknow and presented before a special CBI court from where his transit remand was sought. He was next flown to Delhi and from there brought to Bhopal. On 20 March, Tabish was presented before the Indore court and the CBI obtained his custody for the next ten days.

The second son of Matin Bandookwala, Tabish too had a fascination for guns since he was a child. Tabish's father, Matin, was called Bandookwala because he worked at a gun factory. Tabish had dropped out of school at a very young age and had become involved in petty crimes in Kanpur. He liked to stay in the company of gangsters and criminals and took pride in carrying a gun. Enamoured by Shakib's crime record in Bhopal, Tabish became close to his cousin. Tabish, like Shakib, aspired to earn a big name for himself in the world of crime some day.

Eleven

The Killer's Confession

On the evening of 20 March, Irfan and Tabish were brought face-to-face with each other for the first time. Now that Irfan had already told the whole story, Tabish was forced to accept the role that he had played in the murder.

He admitted that he had been in Bhopal in August 2011. Shakib's cousin, Riyaz, had already confirmed to the CBI, 'Tabish is Shakib's maternal cousin and he had stayed at my house in Shahjahanabad for around twenty days in August 2011.'

Tahir alias Shahid had got the bike to Tabish on Shakib's directions and Tabish admitted that it was he who had driven the black-coloured Bajaj Pulsar bike on 16 August. CBI officers took Tahir to the house on BGBT College Road from where he had picked up the bike. The house belonged to Shadab Khan, who ran a gym and a marriage hall from there. On the first floor, he lived with his family.

Shadab did not take much time to admit his role. 'In August 2011, during the month of Ramzan, Shakib, whom I know since my childhood, borrowed my bike. Tahir came to pick up the bike, MP04 MN 6651. It is registered in the name of my brother-in-law Akbar Khan. Though it belongs to my brother-in-law, I always use it. The bike was returned to me after ten to twelve days,' he recalled.

Tabish's phone numbers were already with the CBI and their movement was being tracked. Keshav Kumar and his team had now gathered enough forensic evidence to prove that Tabish had indeed travelled to Bhopal in August 2011.

By this time, Irfan had already given up and named Tabish as the one he was trying to save on Shakib's directions. He now wanted to record his statement before a magistrate under Section 164 of the Criminal Procedure Code. Tabish was convinced that his game was up and knew the statement could be used as evidence against him in court.

The CBI was again convinced that the case was sealed. Irfan was presented before the Indore court on 22 March and remanded to fifteen days of judicial custody. At the same time, the CBI moved an application seeking isolation for Irfan. 'He has expressed the desire to give a confessional statement under Section 164 of the CrPC (criminal procedure code) and therefore he should be kept away from the others for at least the next twenty-four hours. They can apply undue pressure on him to change his mind,' the CBI said in its application before the court. The judge issued the required orders and 24 March was appointed as the date for the recording of Irfan's statement under Section 164.

On the assigned day, Irfan was presented before the court at around 11.00 a.m. Dr Shubra Singh, the special magistrate for all CBI cases in Indore, was already sitting in her chair. She asked all the advocates and policemen guarding Irfan to leave the court. Only three people were present in the court. Singh, her reader-cum-typist and Irfan. Irfan had spent the previous twenty-four hours in isolation in jail. He had now firmly made up his mind to give his confessional statement.

Singh explained to Irfan that he was not bound to give a confessional statement under section 164. 'Once the statement is given, it can be used as evidence against you,' she said to Irfan. For the next two hours, Singh asked questions and Irfan replied to all of them, while the typist keyed in each word.

Singh (SS): How many siblings do you have?

Irfan: We are four sisters and three brothers. One brother is elder to me, the other is younger to me. My two sisters are married, while two are unmarried and they are younger to me.

SS: How many criminal cases are pending against you?

Irfan: Three criminal cases are pending against me in Kanpur.

SS: How do you know Tabish?

Irfan: The accused Tabish lives in my neighbourhood, Talak Mahal Lal Kuan, Kanpur.

SS: For how long have you known Tabish?

Irfan: As we live in the same locality, I know him since my childhood.

SS: How do you know Shakib?

Irfan: I had first met Babloo in the Kanpur jail. He is also called Babloo Chonga. Sometime around the year 2007, I met Babloo again. He asked me to accompany him to Bhopal. I went with him to Bhopal in connection with the shoe-slipper business. He showed me around Bhopal and also took me to Shakib. He told me that Shakib was a builder. Babloo had gone to him looking for a house after getting married. Shakib had kept several animals at his house like two-three dogs, sheep, and pigeons. Thereafter, whenever I was in Bhopal I used to stay at Babloo's house. During my spare time, I would visit Shakib's house.

SS: Before this particular incident when did you meet Shakib the last time?

Irfan: My two sisters Noor Fatima and Nisha Noor were getting married. I had gone to Babloo with a fresh stock of shoes. I used to buy shoes-slippers from the wholesale market in Kanpur and hand them over to Babloo, who would then sell them and give me the money from the sale. This must be somewhere around one month before the murder. I kept the stock that I had taken to Bhopal with Babloo and went to see Shakib. I asked him if he could lend me anything about Rs 50,000 to Rs 1 lakh. He refused and I asked him if he could help me in arranging the money from somewhere else. He said he would let me know whenever it was possible. The next day I returned to Kanpur.

SS: When and how did Shakib contact you in connection with this particular incident?

Irfan: This happened almost fifteen days before the murder. Amir, the elder brother of Tabish came to our house in Kanpur and informed my parents about Shakib's telephone call. My name is Irfan alias Shyam. At my home, he said, 'Tell Shyam to talk to Shakib.' I don't stay with my parents after my marriage, but I used to go there once in a while in the evenings to see my father, who was not keeping well. That day, when I went to my father's house, my sister told me,

'Matin's son had come and he has asked to you to talk to Shakib.' After listening to this I went straight to Amir's shop in Begumganj. He told me that Shakib had called. He gave me a telephone number and asked me to call on it. I spoke to Shakib that very moment. He said, 'Wherever you are and in whatever condition you are, just leave whatever you are doing and come to Bhopal. Your money has been arranged.' I told him I didn't have the money for the train ticket. He said, 'Borrow it from someone but come over.'

SS: After how many days did you come to Bhopal to meet Shakib?

Irfan: The very next day I borrowed Rs 500 from my mother and reached Bhopal; even though she did not have the money, she borrowed it from someone and gave it to me. I took the Pushpak Express to Bhopal. At around 6.00-6.30 a.m. I spoke to Shakib. He asked me to go to Babloo's house and see him later during the day. At Babloo's house I freshened up and had tea and went to see Shakib at his house around 10.00 a.m.

SS: After that what transpired between you and Shakib?

Irfan: Shakib did not tell me anything at that time. He drove me in his car to a place where Tabish had already reached before us. Tabish sat in the car and we started moving around. They then took me around to the place where the incident had happened. At that time, I thought they were perhaps looking for someone who they wanted to meet. After some time, Tabish got dropped at the spot from where we had picked him up from. The two of us went to Shakib's house and had lunch. While having lunch, he told me to come again the next day morning. He assured me that he would soon tell me about the person from whom the money had been arranged.

SS: When did he tell you about the task?

Irfan: The next day, Tabish took me to the same spot. I was made to stand near the actual spot when a lady crossed in her car. Tabish said she is the madam. I asked, what about this madam? Tabish was surprised and said, 'Shakib has not told you anything?' Tabish too did not tell me anything at that time. I immediately called up Shakib from the phone that he had given me and he came to where we were. I asked him why they were making me move around this particular spot like this. 'Have you arranged the money for me or not?' I asked. Shakib said, 'I will take care of the money required for your sisters but you have to kill the madam you just saw.' I replied, 'I did not see the madam properly and also I cannot kill.' Shakib told me, 'In that case the money cannot be arranged. And if you cannot arrange the money it will reflect badly on your honour.' Somehow, I gathered the courage and asked him to show me the madam's face. The next day, the three of us, Tabish, Shakib and I reached the road in front of the spot by Shakib's car. We parked the car on one side. Madam was drying her hair then. At that time, again I could not see her face properly but I fibbed and said that I had seen it.

SS: Did these people tell you the name of madam?

Irfan: No, they did not tell me the name of madam. They also did not tell me whether she was a Hindu or a Muslim.

SS: Did those people tell you why they wanted to kill madam?

Irfan: I had asked Shakib and he told me, 'This madam takes tuitions and supplies the girls coming to her to study to politicians.' When I refused to believe, he called someone and put the phone on speaker. There was a lady on the other side, who also repeated the same thing.

SS: How did you execute the murder?

Irfan: The next day I met Tabish. Shahid got a black-coloured Pulsar. This motorcycle was given to me and Tabish to commit the murder. The two of us left for the spot on the bike. Shakib followed us in his car. Madam's car crossed me. I was scared then and so I returned from the spot. Shakib also followed me to ask what had happened. I told him I could not gather the courage. After this I made an excuse in front of Shakib that I had to appear in a court case in Kanpur. I said I will return after getting a new date and I also asked him for money. He gave me Rs 3,000 and I went back to Kanpur. After around three, four or five days after attending my court date I was trying to arrange money so I did not have to return to Bhopal. Shakib was continuously calling me and asking when I was coming to Bhopal. Three-four days passed but I could not arrange for the money. After this I decided to come to Bhopal. Tabish had asked me to get his clothes from his brother Danish. I went to Tabish's house and Danish gave me two shirts and trousers for Tabish and one shirt for me. I took the Pushpak Express again to Bhopal. On reaching Bhopal, I went to Babloo's house and kept the clothes there and from there left to go to Shakib's. When I called up Shakib, he said he was coming on a two-wheeler to pick me up. We went to see Tabish. Babloo came along with me to meet Tabish. Tabish was surprised to see Babloo and asked me why I had brought him along. Babloo was carrying hashish with him, which all three of us smoked. From there we went to Shakib's house on a two-wheeler. We had food at Shakib's house and then went to Babloo's house to sleep.

The next day, I went back to Shakib's house, who took me in his car. He called up Shahid and asked him to get the motorcycle to the place where we were to meet Tabish.

Shahid left after handing over the motorcycle. Tabish gave me a .315-bore country-made gun. Shakib had given this weapon to Tabish, who in turn gave it to me. The gun was loaded with one bullet. I was given three other bullets, which I had kept in my pocket. We reached madam's house on the motorcycle and Shakib reached behind us in a car. Shakib was on one side while we were on the other.

Madam came out of the house, sat in her car and left in front of me. I could not gather the courage and we came back to the spot where Tabish used to meet us. Shakib also came there, and I told him I did not have the courage and also I had not seen her properly. He said that we will go in the evening and see when she returns.

That evening we went again. It was raining and madam had not come home. We called up Shakib and he informed us that he was chasing her and that she had gone somewhere. He asked us to come over to his house. I went along with Tabish to the spot where we used to meet, and from there went to Babloo's house.

The next day I wore Tabish's shirt and went to Shakib's house. Shahid joined us there and took out the motorcycle after taking the keys from Shakib. Shahid started asking why the motorcycle was being taken out like this again and again. Shakib told him that I (Shyam) had come to see Bhopal and Tabish was showing me around. After this, I sat in the car and Shakib took me to the place where Tabish used to meet us. There was an aata-chakki [flour mill] at this place. Shahid also came here and Tabish took the bike from him. I sat pillion behind him, and again he handed over the loaded gun to me. He gave me three more bullets to keep in my pocket. We went to the spot where madam used to park her car. I got down from the motorcycle and stood behind the car while Tabish stopped the bike at about ten to twelve feet from the car. When madam got out of the house and sat in her car, Tabish gave me a signal and after seeing madam I behaved as if I did not know him. Madam reversed her car and came onto the road from where she used to leave. After this, Tabish parked his motorcycle in front of the car and I moved in front of the car a couple of times and since I did not want to kill her I signalled to Tabish to move his motorcycle. Madam was also honking at him and she negotiated her way and moved ahead. Tabish started blaming me.

SS: How many times did you go to try and kill that madam?

Irfan: We went four-five times to kill madam but I could not do it. By now, Shakib and Tabish were getting more and more angry with me and were also abusing me.

SS: What happened on the day when madam was killed?

Irfan: On the day of the murder, we reached the spot near the aata-chakki shop. Shakib was also there and standing by the road. Tabish told us that some accident had happened and that the police were coming. He said we should get away from the spot quickly. I got scared and gave the weapon and bullets back to Tabish. After this I sat in the car. I was really scared. I had smoked hashish. I went to Babloo's house and changed my shirt. My shirt was lying there. It was only later that I came to know that the name of the madam whom Shakib had asked me to kill was Shehla Masood.

SS: Did you know that the lady who was being shown to you again and again and the one whom you were asked to kill was Shehla Masood?

Irfan: I cannot tell whether the person who I was seeing again and again was the same person. I had seen her photo on television. The news was being repeated through which I came to know that her name was Shehla Masood.

SS: Did you ask Shakib who committed this murder?

Irfan: I was very scared. Shakib gave me Rs 5,000 and asked me to leave for Kanpur. He also told me that he would bear the expenses of the marriage of my sisters. He also told me that nothing had happened with my hands and that I should forget everything. I had gone to commit murder, but the murder had already been committed so I was very scared. I left for Kanpur.

SS: After the incident, how much money did Shakib give you?

Irfan: Shakib gave me Rs 35,000, and that too after I threatened to come to Bhopal and tell everything to the police. Shakib gave this money after almost fifteen days of the incident when I had come to his house.

SS: You never asked him why he was giving money to you as you had not done the job?

Irfan: I required the money so I did not ask anything.

SS: Can you tell who could have committed this murder?

Irfan: Shakib and Tabish both were on the spot. Who pulled the trigger I cannot say. I had given the weapon to Tabish and he had given it to Shakib, but it has still not been recovered. Shakib and Tabish are into this business.

SS: Why did the CBI arrest you?

Irfan: Shakib explained to me and said, 'The CBI is enquiring and I will have to give a statement. If you say as I instruct you to, we will keep sending money to your wife. You have to go to jail on some warrant.' Shakib had surrendered before the CBI in Delhi. He told the same story to the CBI. Shakib took my name and the CBI arrested me. I have not committed any

> crime. I was lodged in Kanpur jail. The police had picked me from my home.

At the end of this lengthy question-answer session, the entire statement was once again read out to Irfan and he accepted it to be true.

The CBI was hoping to seal the case with Irfan's statement, but it was not to be. He had stopped short of accepting what he had told the investigators in CBI custody; that he had pulled the trigger.

The investigators however were happy that he had nearly said everything that Kumar and Bothra were trying to prove through the technical evidence that they had gathered. Shakib and Irfan had initially tried to mislead the investigators by taking Shanoo Olanga's name, who was already dead, but their bluff had been exposed. They were happy that now it had been proved beyond doubt that Irfan, Tabish and Shakib had gone to attempt to kill Shehla several times, and had finally shot her on 16 August.

The next target was to get the weapon used to commit the murder. Everything else was in place. Irfan in his statement had said that he had given the weapon to Tabish. Tabish was now saying that he had given it to Shakib. Shakib was in judicial custody and there was no way in which he could be questioned in jail. The CBI tried to send a message to him in jail but he was being smart. He knew that if the weapon were to be recovered from him, he would be nailed.

The CBI once again went back to the Bhopal police. They wanted to find out if there were any pending cases for which Shakib's questioning was required. The idea behind this was to get Shakib out of prison on some pretext and question him about the weapon used in the murder. The Bhopal police outrightly refused saying that there were no pending cases for which Shakib's questioning was required.

The weapon was yet to be recovered. The CBI officers discreetly sent a message to Shakib that the UP STF had moved a file to seek his remand in connection with a weapon that they had recovered from Irfan. The weapon had allegedly been supplied to Irfan by Shakib. The CBI messenger also told him that a file had already moved and had reached the Kanpur district collector, whose signature was required. Shakib was told that the investigators wanted to take out their frustration as he had fooled them for a long time now and that it was in fact the CBI that had chalked out this plan just so he could be properly questioned to recover the weapon.

Shakib knew that if the UP STF were granted his custody, he would be subjected to the third degree and there was no way in which he could hide the weapon of offence any more then. The first thing that he did on the morning of 4 March was to send a message through one of his visitors that the weapon had been carefully packed and hidden in the pigeon house on the roof of his house.

A team immediately left for Shakib's house. As he had said, the weapon was found in a plastic bag inside the pigeon house on his roof. The weapon had been recovered but it needed to be checked by the CFSL. The investigators no longer trusted Shakib and now they wanted the shell of the cartridge that was recovered from Shehla's body.

Now that the weapon used in the crime had been recovered, the new challenge was to connect the dots on paper. Irfan had said so many things in his confessional, but his claims had to be backed by evidence. The investigators started with Tabish. Where had he stayed when he had come to Bhopal in February?

He named Shakib's cousin, Riyaz. Riyaz was immediately called and he confirmed that Tabish had come to his house in February.

Tabish was asked to narrate everything that had happened during his second visit to Bhopal. He was asked to repeat the same thing over and over again. The investigators wanted to exhaust him and see if there was any inconsistency in his story.

Tabish finally confessed that he and Shakib had together planned the Shanoo Olanga theory. He said that he had heard about Shanoo's death and seen the picture of Raees Banarsi killing him outside the Kanpur court. He tossed the idea to Shakib, who was excited about it and the two then went back to Kanpur to take Irfan into confidence. In their meeting with Irfan they convinced him to keep Tabish out of the whole story. Irfan fell into the trap and thought that since Olanga was dead, he too would escape criminal liability and would be out of jail after a short stint. The two also explained to Irfan that the CBI had already announced a reward of Rs 10 lakh on the case, which they would claim through the person who would present them before the CBI.

Tabish told the investigators that they had travelled back to Kanpur by the Gareeb Rath train on 19 February on a third-AC ticket. To confirm this, all third-AC tickets booked from Bhopal to Kanpur on the Gareeb Rath train on 19 February were checked. A ticket in the name of a Shahid and Laeek was found for 19 February. Shahid and Laeek were summoned and they admitted that the tickets were booked in their names, but Tabish and Shakib had travelled in their place.

The address given on the reservation slip of this ticket was 16, Kachhi Saray, near railway station, Bajaria, Bhopal. A team was immediately dispatched to this address. This place belonged to a former hockey player, who now worked with the Bharat

Heavy Electricals Limited. His name was Salim. His call details suggested that he was in regular touch with Shakib.

Salim was immediately picked up and brought to the CBI office in Bhopal. Salim admitted that he had booked the tickets for Tabish and Shakib through Bunty who operated from platform number one at the railway station. Salim also admitted that the tickets were booked in the names of Shahid and Laeek, but Tabish and Shakib were the ones who had boarded the train in their place.

The next to be picked up was Bunty. He was shown the reservation slip. He accepted that it was his handwriting and explained the sequence of events as they had occurred.

'Salim had called me on the 17 or 18 of February. He said that he wanted two tickets for Kanpur for his friends for the same day. I said it was impossible, but I told him that he could get a ticket for Sunday. Salim agreed and gave me Shahid and Laeek's names. I wrote the names on the reservation slip and against the address column I wrote 16, Kachhi Saray, near railway station, Bajaria, Bhopal. This is Salim's address. I had also written the train number 12594 on the reservation slip. One of my boys got the ticket confirmed and signed on the slip.

'On 19 February, as Salim had said, a man came to collect the tickets. I did not know who he was. He gave me Rs 950 for the tickets.'

Laeek, a friend of Shakib's who used to drive his car, also confirmed to the CBI that he had dropped Tabish and Shakib at the railway station before they left for Kanpur by the Gareeb Rath train on 19 February.

The CBI now knew how Shakib had planned his own surrender and tried to fool the leading investigating agency of the country. The question as to why Shakib planned his surrender was also equally important if not more.

Twelve

Why Shakib Planned His Own Surrender

While gathering information about Shakib, it was found that he was using two numbers: 9300xxxxxx and 9993xxxxxx. All the numbers that were collected by the CBI were run through the database of the nine lakh numbers that Keshav Kumar and his team had so diligently developed. Kumar and Bothra found the number 9300xxxxxx present in the tower dump of Koh-e-Fiza on three days; 14, 16 and 17 August 2011.

All the numbers that Shakib had called and the numbers from which he had received calls were also run through the system. The CBI received another breakthrough when they found the number 9301xxxxxx, a regular contact of Shakib's, in the Koh-e-Fiza tower dump. The number was also present in the area outside Shehla's house on the day that she was murdered. This number was registered in the name of Tahir Khan, son of Sabbir Khan, a resident of 8/8 PGBT college, Bhopal.

A team was sent to the address and briefed to discreetly gather all available information about him.

Tahir Khan was known as Shahid in the locality and he worked as a school bus driver. He had never gone to school and had married a Hindu girl. In his spare time, he organized ram fights.

The CBI officials now approached the school where he worked and found that he had another mobile number, 8871xxxxxx. This number was registered in the name of Shahid Khan, son of Sabbir Khan, who again was a resident of 8/8 PGBT college.

The school bus driver was shadowed for twenty-four hours. The school bus' route was also checked. It did not go anywhere near Koh-e-Fiza. The school confirmed that Tahir alias Shahid was on duty on 16 August. The question then was: who had been in Koh-e-Fiza on the same day, carrying the number registered in Tahir's name?

The investigators decided to approach Tahir. They went to his house early one morning when he was about to leave for work. 'We have come from a telecom company, as a number registered in your name has won a cash award. We need your identity documents to cross-check with the papers that you had submitted when you had bought the SIM card. The problem is that we have found two people with the same papers.'

Tahir said that both identities were his. The investigators asked, 'Why did you use two identities to buy two different numbers?' Tahir told them that one of his numbers was being used by his friend's wife and wanted to know which number had won the cash award.

The investigators had done their homework and knew which number he used. 'The number which your friend's wife is using is the one that has won the cash prize. But, since it is registered in your name, you will get the award,' they said and asked him to pose for photographs with his identification papers.

In the meanwhile, another CBI team was tasked with shadowing him. That same night, the officer keeping a watch on him informed the CBI that Tahir had gone to Shakib's house.

The call detail report (CDR) analysis of Shakib and Tahir's numbers threw up yet another interesting aspect. Shakib's number had been a regular visitor to Koh-e-Fiza, while the number registered in Tahir's name had visited Koh-e-Fiza for the first time at 9.54 a.m. on 11 August.

Next, Kumar and Bothra did a comparative analysis of Shehla's CDR and Tahir's CDR. The results were very pleasing to the two officers and they knew that they were moving in the right direction.

On 11 August, Shehla's number had left the Koh-e-Fiza tower a little after 10.54 a.m., while Tahir's number had entered the Koh-e-Fiza area at 9.54 a.m. and left the tower a little after 10.56 a.m.

Through this, the investigators could conclude that Shehla was being watched as the person who had been carrying Tahir's number had left the spot minutes after she had left her house.

On 12 August, the pattern was repeated. Tahir's number entered the Koh-e-Fiza tower at 10.33 a.m. and left a little after 11.50 a.m., minutes after Shehla had left her house after 11.43 a.m. that day.

The CDR of the phone number revealed that on the day of the murder, it had called the toll-free number 367 fifty-seven times while it was in Sector 2 of the Koh-e-Fiza tower. The Koh-e-Fiza tower is located a few houses away from Shehla's and the tower's Sector 2 covers the area right in front of these houses.

A little after the incident on 16 August, Tahir's number had been switched off. It had been switched on again only on 19 August at 6.45 p.m. at Nishatpura.

The route taken by the phone numbers belonging to Shakib and Tahir on 16 August was mapped out on Google Maps by the investigators, with assistance from the mobile company officials. A pattern emerged and the same was shown through a PowerPoint presentation to the CBI director in Delhi.

Armed with Shakib and Tahir's CDRs, which showed some common Kanpur contacts, Bothra left for Kanpur. There, he and DSP Triveni Singh started working on the numbers that Shakib and Tahir were in touch with. All the numbers moved in and around the Begumganj area. The task now was to identify the people who carried these numbers and establish their relationship with the two Bhopal numbers under suspicion.

Shakib, who was on the run after realizing that the CBI was zeroing in on him, found out that the CBI had come to look for him at his house; he knew that sooner or later he would be caught. He called up Zahida and told her that the CBI was zeroing in on him and that he had got nothing from her except a little money. Zahida knew what he was angling at. She called him to the Maulana Azad National Institute of Technology (MANIT) saying that a room was available there. Shakib called his friend Raees and asked him to accompany him, saying that Zahida would be accompanied by her friend. It was meant to be an orgy.

On the given day, while driving towards MANIT, an excited Shakib called up Zahida. They had reached the gate of the institute when Raees got suspicious. From the voices that he heard on the phone, he could sense that someone else was giving directions to the woman speaking on the phone. Raees refused to go and asked Shakib to stop the car. He advised Shakib not to go, saying that he sensed that something was not well. Shakib heeded Raees' advice.

After a while, Zahida called him. She wanted to know where he was. 'I just got a call from a friend. He needs urgent help and I have to go, so I will not be able to come today. I will call you later and we will fix up a meeting,' Shakib said. Zahida was disappointed and almost pleaded with him to come to the designated spot.

On the way back from MANIT, Raees was curious. He did not understand why Zahida was so anxious to see him. Shakib told him the entire story. How he had gone to meet her at her MP Nagar office in connection with recovering the money that she owed to Faiz, and how he had fallen for her, how she had been teasing him and the messages that she had been sending him. Raees raised some doubts, 'Why has it been taking so long for you to lay this woman? She is not the first woman in your life and why has she finally agreed now?' Raees and Shakib now realized that they had just narrowly escaped. A plan to eliminate the most crucial link in the Shehla Masood murder case had just been foiled.

Raees, a 5 feet 5 inches tall father of three girls, had earned the alias 'Scientist'. The first time that he saw a school building from the inside was when he had gone along with his wife to get his eldest daughter admitted. At a very young age, he had become a motorcycle mechanic's apprentice from whom he had learnt everything about repairing motorcycles. Soon, he became excellent at the job and could repair engines that no one else could. He started innovating and fixed old motorcycle engines onto damaged bikes and sold them off to youngsters at a very low cost. People in his fraternity started calling him 'Scientist' for his creative skills; he did not know how to copy a number from a mobile phone onto a piece of paper but give him a faulty engine and he would bring it to life. Raees Scientist, like Shakib, had a passion for ram fights. The two became friends after organizing many such fights.

Shakib told Raees how the CBI investigators had reached his house while investigating the Shehla Masood murder. While they drove in the old city area, Shakib told Raees that he had arranged for the killers to eliminate Shehla Masood through his cousin Tabish, and that Irfan had come from Kanpur to execute the killing. And that he had just got Rs 3 lakhs from Zahida Parvez. Shakib told Raees that he had demanded more money from Zahida after the CBI had raised the reward to Rs 10 lakhs. Raees now figured why Zahida had been so desperate to meet Shakib at the MANIT campus. He was furious but the two now hatched a plan – they would fix Zahida and take the reward money as well.

They then fixed the deal. Raees would ensure a safe surrender and Shakib would fix up things with Tabish and Irfan in Kanpur. The prize money would be equally split between Raees and Shakib. Raees knew that it was not safe for Shakib to stay in Bhopal; it was just a matter of time before he was located by the CBI. Their first job was to ensure a safe house for Shakib and then to move him out of Bhopal at the earliest. He did not want Shakib to travel alone, so Tabish was immediately called. The two then went to a common friend's place which they thought was safe for the night.

The next day, Tabish came to Bhopal. He went straight to the house where he had stayed in August.

On 18 February 2012, Shakib Danger, Raees Scientist, Laeek and Tabish went to the Govindpura house of hockey player Salim Ahmed in a silver-coloured Tata Indigo car. Raees had sorted out the surrender plan. The first thing required was to move Shakib and Tabish out of Bhopal.

Shakib asked Salim to arrange for two train tickets to Kanpur. Salim immediately called up his agent Bunty, who said he could arrange tickets only for the next day. But Shakib was impatient to leave immediately. He told Raees that he and Tabish would leave in the general compartment without any reservation, but Raees refused. He wanted to keep a record; a trail that could be accessed later, if need be. So Shakib had no other option but to agree to the plan to leave the next day on 19 February.

For the night, they asked Salim to arrange for a place where they could relax and party outside Bhopal. Laeek went back in the Tata Indigo car and Shakib, Raees, Tabish and Salim left for a dam in Raisen district in a Gypsy. They halted for the night at a friend's farm in Raisen, where they thought no one could trace them. They drank till midnight and returned to Bhopal only by noon the next day.

On their return Raees took Tabish along with him, and Salim and Shakib went to the Sindhi market, where they released their tension by organizing a ram fight. As decided earlier, Raees and Tabish came with Laeek in the car to Salim's Govindpura house in the evening and after picking up Salim and Shakib, they went to the railway station, where Bunty handed them the tickets.

As Shakib and Tabish boarded the train to Kanpur, Raees asked Shakib to wait for his next call and to not disclose the plan to anyone else.

From the railway station, Raees went to meet the owner of a hotel; he had already fixed an appointment with him for the evening. With the help of his contact, he wanted to meet a former SP of Bhopal, who was an IPS officer from the batch of 1990.

The next morning, the two went to the IPS officer's home and after narrating the entire story, requested him to connect them to a top official in the CBI. The officer first confirmed that the story was plausible and that he was not being fooled. Satisfied, the officer called up a senior of his, an IPS officer of the MP cadre from the batch of 1988, and repeated the story that Raees Scientist and the hotel owner had told him. The senior officer spoke to Raees Scientist on the phone and asked him to come to Delhi immediately.

Before leaving for Delhi, Raees Scientist dictated a letter to his eleven-year-old daughter, in which he gave the details of his travel plans to Delhi, and also outlined Shakib and Tabish's travel details. Raees also asked his daughter to write down all the numbers which he had earlier spoken to and mentioned in clear words the purpose of his visit. He asked his daughter to release the contents of the letter to the media if he failed to call within the next two days. Raees' daughter started crying and asked him why he was getting himself entangled in such a deal. He smiled, but could not tell her that it was a question of Rs 10 lakhs, the reward that the CBI had declared to nab the perpetrators of Shehla Masood's murder.

In Delhi, the officer took Raees straight to the special director of the CBI, Salim Ali. Ali listened to Raees and asked him to immediately call Shakib to Delhi. Raees called Shakib up, with the phone being on speaker. All senior CBI officers were listening in. 'Shakib, I'm at the CBI office. I have spoken about your surrender. They want to know how you executed the murder.' Shakib refused to divulge any details on the phone and said, 'I will narrate everything face-to-face.' He then took a train to Indore and from there went to Delhi. As advised by Raees, he kept a record of his travels.

Once Shakib landed in Delhi, he was taken to meet Ali. AGL Kaul, the new investigating officer on the case was also present in the room.

Shakib narrated the Shanoo Olanga story to Ali and Kaul and revealed how Zahida Parvez had given him a contract to kill Shehla Masood. Later, Kaul himself interrogated both Raees and Shakib and, after he was satisfied with their claims, he reported back to Salim Ali. Shakib and Raees were lodged in a private hotel and a guard kept watch outside the hotel with the instruction that they were not to be allowed to leave the hotel.

Inside, Raees Scientist and Shakib Danger were allowed to have the best of everything and were having a blast.

Ali then called up Kumar and Bothra; Bothra was asked to come back from Kanpur immediately.

Once Bothra arrived, Shakib was once again asked to narrate the whole story. He started from Zahida's call. 'Zahida called me and asked me to come to her office the next day. This was about twenty days before the incident. She showed me a file of newspaper cuttings. She showed me a picture of Shehla Masood and said that she supplied innocent girls to politicians and had also had an affair with her husband. She asked me if I could help her eliminate Shehla Masood. After thinking over what she had told me, I agreed to do the job for Rs 3 lakhs. Her employee showed the location of the Masood house to my friend, who then showed it to me. After that, I contacted Irfan from Kanpur, who needed money for his sister's wedding. Irfan, in turn, spoke to Shanoo Olanga and one Salim. They came to Bhopal and executed the murder on 16 August.'

Shakib gave Irfan's address and telephone number in Kanpur. He also told the CBI that when in Bhopal, Olanga and his team had used Tahir's mobile number. He went on to narrate how he had coordinated with Irfan after the murder and the number on which he had called Zahida.

After cross-checking with the telephone loop, Triveni Singh's team was informed in Kanpur about Shanoo Olanga and Irfan. They put their team on the job to locate Irfan, but he was not to be found at his house. They also found out that Shanoo Olanga had been killed. By now, the CBI had also put Zahida Parvez under surveillance in Bhopal. They knew that once she was picked up, the news would spread like wildfire. The efforts to get hold of Irfan were intensified; even his parents did not know where he lived.

Finally, on 28 February 2012, the top brass in the CBI decided to go in for the kill, as they were worried that Zahida would flee Bhopal if she found out that she had been kept under surveillance by the CBI.

At around noon, the investigators in Bhopal were asked to find out if Zahida was in her office. A constable, who had earlier seen her at the petrol pump that she owned, was sent to her office on the pretext that he wanted to get his house designed. The constable met Zahida and told her that he had come to find out if she would be available in the evening as he wanted to get his wife along with him to plan the interiors of their newly purchased house. Zahida told him that she would be in her office throughout the day and he could bring his wife any time after 3.00 p.m.

The message was conveyed to Delhi and within the next fifteen to twenty minutes, the CBI officers in Bhopal were asked to mobilize a force to raid her office. Lady police officers from the police force were called in to help the CBI.

At around 3.00 p.m., Delhi gave the go-ahead and the force raided Zahida's office. She was informed about her arrest and her office was immediately sealed.

At around 6.00 p.m., Kaul flew to Bhopal with Shakib in tow. Before Shakib boarded the plane, he extracted a promise from the CBI that he would be made an approver in the case and that no one would physically touch him till he remained in CBI custody.

The same day in Kanpur, Triveni Singh and his team kept a vigil outside Irfan's father's house. They were expecting him to come to meet his parents. Around 9.00 p.m. Irfan was arrested under Section 307 of the Indian Penal Code for opening fire on the UP STF team.

Raees Scientist, the man who had planned the entire surrender drama, took the train to Bhopal immediately after Shakib's official arrest.

Raees staked his claim on the Rs 10 lakh award that the two had privately agreed to share among themselves. How and when this would be done would be decided once the CBI gave them the reward money.

And if the CBI did not keep its promise, Raees had kept his own train tickets, Shakib and Tabish's train tickets from Bhopal to Kanpur, and Shakib's train tickets from his Kanpur-Delhi journey. This, he thought, was sufficient for the media to blow up any claims the CBI would put forward about cracking the case.

Thirteen

The CBI Fight over Darbar's Role

Darbar moved an application in the special CBI court in Indore on 23 March 2012. His plea was to bring on record the fact that he had appeared at the CBI headquarters in Delhi on 14 March, the day Zahida had recorded her statement before the court.

'The CBI asked me to appear at its Delhi office for the polygraph test on 14 March. After some preliminary procedure and formal questioning, I was informed that it was not possible to conduct the test because of my ill health and the test was therefore deferred,' he wrote in his application.

Within twenty-four hours of filing this application, Darbar received a call from the CBI. He was required to appear at the headquarters in Delhi the next day. His polygraph test had been rescheduled for 25 March.

Unknown to Darbar, the CBI had deliberately deferred the polygraph test because of Zahida's statement before the magistrate which was supposed to be a confessional of sorts. The CBI did not trust Zahida. Moreover, she had not backed her allegations with any evidence and the CBI did not want to take any chances.

Zahida had alleged that Darbar had given her the money, which she had handed over to the killers. Inspector Sangwan had extracted this information from Zahida while questioning her at the CBI's Bhopal office, the information consequently being passed on to the bosses in Delhi. A faction within the CBI felt there was sufficient evidence to go after Darbar, but another section felt that she could easily turn around her statement later. A statement under Section 164 of the Criminal Procedure Code was the only solution. 'If Zahida sticks to her allegations in her confession under Section 164, Criminal Procedure Code, we will go for Darbar,' the top bosses decided.

Sangwan extended this offer to Zahida. 'Your game is up. You have yourself written about your involvement in your own handwriting in your diary. The killers contacted you immediately after the murder. You met the killers after the murder to give them the money. We have shown you the evidence that we have. If the allegations that you are making against Darbar are true, you will have to make them in front of the magistrate under Section 164. Your fate has been decided, so if you tell the truth before the magistrate, at least the person who used you, as you claim, will not get away.' Zahida had agreed to this proposal. Before this, whenever Zahida was taken to court, she made it a point to level allegations against Darbar to journalists outside the court. But inside the court, she never said a word against him.

On 14 March, in her confessional statement before the magistrate in Indore, Zahida did exactly what the cautious faction within the CBI had suspected. She spoke about her relationship with Darbar, but denied his role in the murder. She also did not say a word about Darbar giving her the money for the alleged killers. Doing so, she knew, would have meant acknowledging her role in the murder conspiracy.

Ready for his next polygraph test, accompanied by his lawyer friend, Darbar left for Delhi by the evening flight on 24 March. The next day, the expert was ready with the questions at the CBI head office. Darbar was made to sit on a chair that had heavy straps attached to it. A gel was applied on his chest and ankles before the straps were fixed onto him. The polygraph was connected to Darbar's heartbeat and immediately reported an abnormality with a beep. The previous evening, a team of CBI officers had okayed the objective questions that were framed in a manner so the truth would come out.

The session started with the most basic questions and was over in twenty minutes. Darbar answered all the questions and denied playing any role in the murder. The machine did not catch any anomalies in his responses. The findings of the polygraph test were, however, kept a closely-guarded secret. Even Darbar was not told anything about it. Off the record, the investigators maintained that the findings of the polygraph test were never conclusive. They only played a limited role in confirming certain things. Also, they admitted, it was possible for hardened criminals to mislead the polygraph machine and the technician monitoring it.

On 26 March, the CBI filed a reply to Darbar's application and sought that his application be set aside on grounds that the application was non-maintainable – the reason that Darbar had no locus standi in the case.

The CBI now was caught in a peculiar situation. More than the opposition party, it was Darbar's own party that wanted him fixed in the Shehla Masood murder case. The CBI's reluctance to arrest Darbar was attributed to his caste and allegiances: 'Darbar has managed the whole thing with the help of a former chief minister of Madhya Pradesh.' Almost everyone, from police officers to politicians to anyone associated with the Shehla Masood murder case, was certain about the role of this politician who had ruled the state for more than five years. Many even went to the extent of speculating about the amount of money Darbar had spent – a staggering Rs 25 to 30 crores.

Even the CBI director was not left out. It was his surname and the community which he belonged to that was attacked: 'When it comes to their caste, the Thakurs are one, irrespective of whichever political party they belong to.'

The intelligence department of Madhya Pradesh police was once again at work. The job at hand was to find the common link between Zahida, Shakib and Darbar.

A first clue was found. On 14 March when Darbar was in Delhi for his first polygraph test, a mobile number registered in Bhopal showed up in Delhi. It was presumed that this might be a link between Darbar and Shakib, and had travelled along with Darbar to Delhi.

Call records for this number were called up and it was found that this person was in touch with both Shakib and Darbar. The papers taken by the telephone company at the time of issuing the number were called in and the owner was traced to be one Sarathe, who owned a salon in Bhopal. Those from the ruling party, who were working to fix Darbar, were excited and boasted in private: 'The connection has been found. Let's see how the CBI denies it now.'

The number and call records were passed on to the CBI. The CBI was quite excited about this new clue, but also annoyed at missing this in the first place. The number still showed up in

Delhi and a team was specially formed to look into the veracity of this claim.

Finally, after wasting an entire day, it was found that the number was actually lying at the CBI's forensic laboratory in Delhi. In the middle of the night, the laboratory in-charge was called to find out how this mobile number that established a connection between Shakib and Darbar had reached Delhi. It eventually turned out to be nothing. The phone had been seized from Zahida's office and had been sent to the lab for examination. And what about Sarathe, the man in whose name the phone number was issued? A CBI team was dispatched to find Sarathe and it was found that these identity documents had been forged by Zahida.

Another dead end, and now there was an uproar to hang Darbar. Even the CBI was not left out. There were calls to bring the supervising officer of the case on record and a new officer with an open mind to be sent to Bhopal to probe Darbar's role in the case.

As a consequence, T Rajah Balaji, the superintendent of police, was appointed to find out if Darbar had indeed played a role in Shehla Masood's murder. Balaji reached Indore on 20 April. On the same day, the CBI moved an application in the special CBI court seeking permission to examine all the five accused in judicial custody.

The Balaji-led team first went to the district jail where Zahida and Sabah were lodged. Balaji first spoke to them separately and later questioned them together. When questioned together, both of them blamed the CBI officers for their plight and claimed that they were innocent. Zahida repeated her allegations and said that Darbar was the mastermind behind the murder and who had used her. She said that she did not have any evidence to prove her claim, and when asked why she had not recorded this statement in her session before the magistrate, she replied, 'I'm not a fool. By doing so, I would have tied the noose around my neck.'

After questioning Zahida and Sabah, Balaji headed straight to the Indore Central Jail. The jail authorities had already received the court order and the three accused, Shakib, Tabish and Irfan were brought before the CBI team.

Irfan was struck with remorse. He said that he did not know what he had done. Tabish too remained silent and answered every question either with a 'yes' or 'no'. The two did not know anything about why Shehla was killed and who wanted her dead. For them everything ended at Shakib.

Lastly, Shakib was brought before Balaji. He had nothing new to offer. He denied any connection between him and Darbar. When Balaji told him that he could get a life imprisonment sentence, Shakib mocked the officer and said, 'Your agency has no other option but to turn me into an approver. That is the only way you can prove your case. And if you don't do that, I will be out on bail the day you file the charge sheet.' Next, Balaji headed straight to Bhopal and parked himself at the Bharat Heavy Electricals Limited (BHEL) guest house. Darbar was the first to be called in for questioning. His questioning went on for over six hours. His only request was to not let the media know about this.

Just to be sure, Balaji spoke to everyone related to the case yet again and went back to Delhi after a week. In his report that was submitted before the CBI director, he noted, 'There is no evidence to prove Darbar's involvement in the killing of Shehla Masood. In the near future, it is highly unlikely that any evidence will surface.' This was the first time that Darbar had got a clean chit in the murder of Shehla Masood. Officially, however, the investigations were open.

The CBI was now preparing the charge sheet that had to be filed before the stipulated ninety-day period deadline after cracking the case and arresting the accused.

The only missing link was the weapon used in the crime. The forensic report had come in and the gun recovered from Shakib's house did not match the bullet recovered from Shehla's body. Shakib had once again fooled the CBI – he had either given up the wrong gun or had tampered with it. The tampering could be proved only once the bullet shell was recovered. There was no way in which the CBI could close the investigation.

Minus the gun, though, the entire story was now in place.

Fourteen

The Complete Picture

The CBI now had a complete picture of the story.

Darbar's fifty-third birthday was fast approaching in July 2011. Zahida wanted to celebrate it in style this year. Hoardings congratulating Darbar on his birthday had sprung up several days in advance at all major intersections in the city. The hoardings carried pictures of senior leaders from Darbar's party alongside him. Pictures of fans and friends also appeared on these hoardings. Overall, it was an occasion to showcase all those who stood by Darbar. Only Zahida's picture was missing from the hoardings. And she wanted to be on them very dearly.

Bhopal has this tradition of politicians putting up their own hoardings and congratulating themselves on their birthdays. Pictures of fans and friends, who are basically party workers, are added to these hoardings to give an impression that they are the ones who are actually behind this public display of adulation. Politicians compete for space on occasions like Holi, Diwali, and Eid, but on birthdays there is no scarcity of space.

On the occasion of his fifty-third birthday, Darbar too did not want to miss any opportunity to occupy the mind of his voters. He, however, was oblivious of what was going on with Zahida, whose mind was completely occupied by him.

Zahida was worried that like the previous two years, she would once again be ignored by him on his birthday. Deep inside she knew that Darbar was a Casanova, who had sexual relations with several other women besides her. She had confronted him with different names on several occasions, but he had denied the allegations each time and sworn his love for her. She knew that he was lying and was looking for evidence to prove him wrong. She had put several of her men on the job. Sabah too was trying to help, but they could not get hold of any evidence.

On 21 June 2011, both Zahida and Sabah had followed Darbar, while he and his friend, Gupta, were on their way to Gupta's office in Vidya Nagar. The two women had to flee when they realized that Darbar and his friend had noticed them following the car. Fortunately, they were wearing helmets, so Darbar did not know it was Zahida who was following him. Zahida and Sabah parked their scooter in a shopping complex and hid inside a public loo when they realized that Darbar and his friend had started following them. They did not want Darbar to know that they were tracking his movements.

Darbar had, however, recognized the scooter parked in the shopping complex. He knew it was Sabah's. Later in the evening, he stopped Zahida near the Tarun Pushkar swimming pool when she was on her way home. 'Why are you following me like this?' he asked. Zahida did not have an answer, but both Durbar and his friend realized that she was getting over-possessive about him.

With his birthday approaching, Zahida decided to keep a close watch on Darbar. Apart from Sabah, Anil Saini, an employee from her petrol pump was also roped in. Saini had been working at the Parvez petrol pump since 2003. He also worked at Zahida's house and at her office. He did all kinds of odd jobs, like filling water and washing utensils. At home, his job was to fill water from the handpump every day, while at office he did dusting and cleaning.

In May 2011, Zahida had fired Saini after he had failed to turn up to fill water at her house one morning. She herself had had to fill the water from the handpump that day. Saini tried to get a job at many places but did not get one. In the end, he had no other option but to return to Zahida, pleading for a job. She refused to listen, but he hung around her office, hoping she would have a change of heart.

The change of heart occurred on 25 July. Around noon, she called him to her room and told him that he could get his job back if he kept a watch on someone in the Char Imli locality. Saini had no other option but to agree. Zahida immediately got up from her chair and the next minute they were driving to Char Imli. She stopped near a tree and pointed out a house to Saini. It was a government bungalow allotted to a doctor, but Darbar lived there. On the first day, Saini was to call Zahida the moment Darbar stepped out of the house.

Saini stood outside Darbar's house for some time and then called Zahida to inform her that he had left the house. Zahida asked him to leave the spot immediately.

On 26 July, Darbar turned fifty-three and his fans and friends celebrated his birthday at his house. Visitors started arriving at around 11.00 a.m. There were politicians, close friends and people from his constituency. He had expressed his inability to meet Zahida, saying that he could not be seen missing from his house when people were coming to wish him.

Though Zahida understood this she wondered if he would go to see someone else. Saini was stationed outside the house, and in the evening he called Zahida and told her that Darbar had not stepped out of the house the whole day. She was relieved, but happiness was still elusive. She could not meet Darbar on his birthday and celebrate it the way she had wanted to. She ordered a cake and cut it for Darbar at her office, and asked Saini to call it a day and leave the spot.

On 27 July 2011, a day after Darbar's birthday, Saini reached the Design Era office at around 12.30 p.m. A furious Zahida came in much later, at around 1.30 p.m. She asked Saini to go to her house, pick up the scooter and call her on her mobile phone. When Saini called her, she asked him to go straight away to Char Imli and call her upon reaching Darbar's house. Saini knew that he would have to spend yet another day doing nothing. He did not like the job one bit, but something was better than nothing, he thought. At least he was getting money for it.

He picked up his favourite brand of chewing tobacco from a cigarette vendor at the entrance of Char Imli and parked Zahida's scooter on the road opposite Darbar's house from where he could see the main gate of the house, before making a call to his boss.

Darbar's drivers and security staff sat right next to the main gate. Saini walked across the street several times, and then went to the nearby tea-stall to have a cup of tea and on his return, posed as a visitor and asked the security staff if Darbar was still at home and begged for an opportunity to talk to him. He told the security guys that he was jobless and required Darbar's recommendation. The security staff advised Saini to wait for Darbar to come out of the house and attempt to talk to him while he sat in the car.

Saini had almost given up. He was about to call Zahida, seeking permission to leave, when Darbar emerged from the house with one more person. Saini acted as if he wanted to talk to Darbar, but he was never close enough. Darbar and his friend were busy discussing something and drove away without noticing him. He went to his scooter across the road and saw Darbar's car take a U-turn and move past him. He now called Zahida to inform her of what he had just seen.

Zahida asked him to follow the car. The car drove straight to Koh-e-Fiza. Zahida called Saini to check on the exact address and location of the car. Saini had no idea about the exact address but he knew that he was in Koh-e-Fiza. 'Tell me the number of the house he has gone into. And if the house number is not written outside, there must be some car parked outside it. Tell me its number,' she shouted at Saini on the phone. Saini quietly went to the Santro that was parked outside the house and read out the number to Zahida.

Sabah was the next to call Saini. She wanted to know the exact spot where Saini stood. Zahida had already instructed her to cross-check everything. Saini had just finished giving directions to Sabah when Darbar came out of the house and sat in his car. Saini tried chasing him but lost him in the traffic.

Back at the office, Zahida was fuming. She could not control her emotions. She called up Darbar and blasted him. Darbar was also angry initially, but gradually tried to reason with her, saying that Doctor was also with him. 'We had gone for some political work,' he said. But Zahida was not one to get convinced so easily.

After crying for over an hour, Zahida turned to what she had been doing regularly for almost three years now. She started her diary entry with the date 27 August 2011, 'I could not talk to Darbar throughout the day today. In the evening, I asked Saini to chase him and dot at 7.00 p.m. both he and Doctor went to meet Shehla at her house. I called Darbar at around 7.45 p.m. and blasted him like anything. I cried a lot. From the other number, I called up Shehla and listened to her for thirty seconds.'

Zahida's diary had shared her pain till now. Every time she wrote something in it, she felt better. Her anger and frustration usually subsided the moment she had finished pouring her heart out. But today it was not to be. Her frustration and anger knew no bounds. She felt broken. The man for whom she had waited the whole day, for whom she had put everything, including her family and two daughters at stake, was now drifting away from her. Inside her head she had already decided. Shehla was the culprit. It was because of Shehla that Darbar was not talking to her, she thought. She was okay with his wife, but she would not allow any other woman to take Darbar away from her. She immediately called up Shakib alias Danger and asked him to see her in her office the next day.

Shakib walked into the Design Era office at around noon on 28 July, where Zahida and Sabah were already waiting for him. After ensuring that the door of her cabin was closed, Zahida threw a file with SM written on it on the table. The file contained newspaper cuttings of the *Hindustan Times* and *Free Press*. Both newspaper clippings were dated 7 April 2011 and carried pictures of anti-corruption activists fasting in support of Anna Hazare, who was on an indefinite fast in Delhi. Both newspaper cuttings had Shehla Masood's picture. 'I want this woman dead. Her name is Shehla Masood. She calls herself an anti-corruption activist, but the reality is that she is a bad influence on girls. She is running a call girl racket. She is also having an affair with my husband.'

Shakib did not know how to react and picked up the file trying to have a closer look at the picture.

'You have been telling me that you can do anything for me. Now tell me, can you arrange to eliminate this woman? I want her dead.' Zahida further added, 'You don't bother about the money.'

Shakib had been involved in a murder case in the past. He had a long criminal history with several cases pending against him, but this was something that he had never ever done before; killing a woman who was allegedly having an affair with the husband of another woman.

'You do this for me and I will do anything for you. Also, you don't worry about money,' Zahida reiterated. Shakib had been flirting with Zahida and fell into the trap. He said that he could do the work for three lakhs and that it was no big deal for him. He left the Design Era office, saying that he would contact her later in the afternoon.

Shakib wanted to know where Shehla lived. Zahida told him that her employee, Saini, had been to Shehla's house the previous day. 'Tell him to reach Koh-e-Fiza hospital at 8.00 p.m. My man, Shahid, will come there on a black scooter. Tell Saini to show the house to him.' Zahida immediately asked Saini to go to the hospital at 8.00 p.m. and asked to report back after his meeting with Shahid.

Shakib asked Shahid, with whom he had drunk many a day away, to take his black scooter from Idris, his driver and go to Koh-e-Fiza to meet Saini and check out the location of the house that Saini would show him. Shahid borrowed the black Honda Activa and drove to Koh-e-Fiza hospital and parked the scooter at a spot between the Bajaj showroom and the hospital. It was already growing dark and there was not much traffic on the main road. Shahid had just emptied a gutka pouch into his mouth while standing next to the black scooter, when a man wearing a blue-coloured uniform approached him. 'Are you

Shahid?' he asked. 'Zahida told me that you will show me the Koh-e-Fiza house,' Shahid replied.

Saini immediately called up Zahida. He then took Shahid to A-100 and pointed out the house which he had seen Darbar enter the previous day. Shahid reached Shakib's house around 9.00 p.m. Over drinks he asked Shakib why he had to see the house. Shakib evaded his question and asked him to concentrate on their evening of revelry.

The next day, Shakib and Shahid went to A-100, Koh-e-Fiza, in a silver-coloured Tata Indigo. Once near the house, Shakib slowed down and noted the number of the car parked outside the house. After dropping Shahid off at his place of work, Shakib called up Babloo Chauka. Babloo was surprised to get a call from Shakib. Shakib had stopped calling and meeting Babloo after he had tried to change his profile to get closer to politicians. When Shakib insisted on meeting immediately, Babloo called him over to his one-room house, where he stayed with his wife.

At the house, after the two shared a smoke, Shakib asked for Irfan's number. 'Irfan had come to me about a month back and asked me for some help in some matter. I could not help him at that time, but now his work is done,' he told Babloo. Babloo did not have Irfan's latest number, but he gave him a number on which he had last spoken to Irfan. Shakib took the number, tried calling on it, but it was switched off. He left the house, telling Babloo to ask Irfan to contact him if he ever met him. Babloo knew that Shakib would not be so desperate to contact Irfan had it not been for his own work.

Next, Shakib got in touch with his cousin Tabish. He knew Irfan and Tabish lived in the same neighbourhood and that it would be the easiest way to get in touch with Irfan. Shakib refused to divulge anything to Tabish. Tabish too did not have

Irfan's contact number, but he knew his father's house where he thought he would be able to get hold of him.

When Irfan was not found anywhere, Shakib asked Tabish to leave for Bhopal and requested his elder brother, Amir, to pass on a one-line message to Irfan: 'Call me ASAP.' Tabish left for Bhopal the next evening. The same evening, Amir went to Irfan's parents' house in Talak Mahal and left a message for him: 'Shakib of Bhopal desperately wants to talk to you. Call him ASAP.'

Shakib received Tabish at the railway station early morning the next day. While driving back from the railway station, an anxious Tabish again asked about the work. 'What is it that you had to call me in such urgency?' he asked. Shakib told him about Zahida's offer. 'I have taken up the task and you have to help me out. Irfan had come to me last month, saying that he needed money desperately for the wedding of his two sisters. He can do anything for money. We have to use him smartly. We just have to locate him, get him to Bhopal, get him stoned and put a gun in his hand. Show him the money and he will pull the trigger.' The deal was struck before they had reached Shakib's house.

On 2 August, sitting in a relative's room in Bhopal, Tabish was calling up people in Kanpur who could help him locate Irfan, when he heard Shakib calling for him at the door. 'Your number is not reachable. I'm trying to contact you since afternoon,' he said, as he sat next to Tabish.

'Irfan got the message I had left through Amir. Today he had come to Amir's shop in Kanpur and called me. I have told him nothing except that money has been arranged for him. What he will have to do to get the money has not been told. I have asked him to come over to Bhopal first. He was saying he did not have money even to come to Bhopal, so I asked him to borrow it from someone. He now knows that he will have money for the wedding of his two sisters. He will be here soon.'

Tabish and Irfan lived in the same neighbourhood in Kanpur. Even though both had known each other since childhood they had not kept in regular touch. The two occasionally met to smoke hashish. He was still not sure if Irfan would come to Bhopal, as Shakib claimed he would.

As Shakib had predicted, Irfan borrowed Rs 500 from his mother and left for Bhopal on 3 August. The next day, he reached Bhopal at around 6.00 a.m. He called up Shakib from the railway station. Shakib, still half asleep, asked Irfan to go to Babloo's house and meet him later around 10.00 a.m.

Babloo was not surprised to see Irfan at his house. He knew Shakib had called him. The two smoked a joint while Babloo's wife made tea for them. Babloo asked him why Shakib was so desperate to meet him, but Irfan knew nothing.

Irfan went to Shakib's house at the appointed time. Shakib took out his car and the two drove up to his cousin Riaz Kashmiri's house from where they picked up Tabish. The three then went to Koh-e-Fiza and parked the car on the incline, about a hundred metres from Shehla's house. Shakib and Tabish spoke in gestures, while Irfan looked at them in amusement. He thought that they were waiting for someone and strolling around to pass time. On the way back, Shakib got down at Kashmiri's house and Shakib took Irfan to his house for lunch. Irfan still did not know why he had been called to Bhopal. He tried asking Shakib, but his standard response was, 'I will let you know when the time comes.'

For the next seven days, Shakib and Tabish indulged Irfan in Bhopal. They took him around and kept telling him that his money was being arranged. Irfan whiled away his time smoking hashish with Tabish and Babloo. When he was not smoking, he was sleeping at Babloo's house. Babloo, now curious about the whole thing, kept asking him why he had been called by Shakib, but there was no answer.

It was around 9 or 10 August when Irfan, while smoking a joint with Babloo as usual, told Babloo that the money would be arranged, and that he would have to fire a gun in the open to get the money. 'It is a property dispute. One party is not vacating some property. A gunshot has to be fired in the air to terrorize them and I will get my money.'

A jealous Babloo said, 'Good if you are making money that easily. But don't forget me. You are sleeping and eating in my room for the past so many days. Share some of the money with me too.'

It was around this time that Shakib gave a local-number phone to Irfan and Tabish to use. The number technically belonged to Shahid but Shakib's wife had been using it.

On Saturday, 11 August, Irfan was told that his money had finally been arranged. To complete his task, he was required to accompany Tabish to Koh-e-Fiza.

Tabish took Irfan to the spot at around 9.50 a.m. on a black-coloured Pulsar motorcycle. They parked the motorcycle near an electric pole about fifty metres from Shehla's house and walked towards the main gate of the house. Shakib also reached the spot, but parked at a little distance from where he could see the two.

Tabish was carrying the mobile phone that Shakib had given them. Shakib called the number at 9.54.30 a.m. to confirm that they had reached the spot.

Irfan and Tabish kept a watch on Shehla's house from a distance of about fifteen metres for a little over an hour. Shehla left her house a little after 10.54 a.m. As she drove out of the lane, Tabish told Irfan, 'This is the woman.'

Within the next two minutes, Shakib called Tabish. He had seen Shehla driving away in her car and wanted to know if Tabish had shown the target to Irfan. Tabish said that he had, but Irfan was still not sure if he would kill the woman.

Shakib was now beginning to get angry. 'You won't get the money if you don't kill this woman. I will take care of the money required for the wedding of your sisters, but for that, you have to kill this woman. I have already given my word to someone. And now if you back out it will not be good for you and your honour.'

Irfan was not ready to murder someone and asked why this woman had to be eliminated in the first place. 'She runs a tuition class. Small girls come to her to study, and she introduces them to politicians. She ruins their lives. And if you don't trust me, listen to this.' Shakib dialled a number and put the phone on speaker saying, 'Please tell me what this woman does.' The voice at the other end repeated the story that Shakib had just told Irfan. Irfan was still not convinced, but he said that he would do it.

The three left the spot and decided to return the next day morning. On 12 August, Shakib, Tabish and Irfan returned to the spot at around 10.30 a.m. The previous day, Shehla had left her house around 10.50 a.m., so it was decided to not reach the spot before 10.30 a.m. – they could not afford to expose themselves in the locality for fear of someone noticing them. The chances of their being recognized after committing the crime increased with the time they spent on the spot. They wanted to finish it quickly. The setting and positions were the same. The only time when Irfan could get the opportunity to shoot Shehla was when she left the main door made of thick iron and walked towards her car. It would take a maximum of ten seconds and Irfan had calculated it in his head. Shehla left her house between 11.43 a.m.

and 11.50 a.m. As she walked out of her house, Irfan stood at a little distance, while Tabish sat on the bike. Shehla opened her car door and sat inside. By the time Irfan reached her, she was already backing her car. Tabish tried to block her way, but she honked at him and drove away.

Shakib was furious at Irfan. He had missed an opportunity again, but there was nothing that he could say on the spot. The three left the place.

The same evening Irfan left for Kanpur. He told Shakib that he had some important work to attend to at home. Shakib gave him Rs 3,000 and Tabish asked him to get his clothes from his house and return at the earliest.

Irfan returned to Bhopal by the Pushpak Express on 15 August. The previous day, in Kanpur, he had gone to Tabish's house and got the clothes for Tabish and for himself. From the railway station, he went straight to Babloo's room. He had just entered the room when he got a call from Shakib and had to leave. Babloo walked with Irfan for some distance and as they reached Riaz Kashmiri's house, he saw Tabish standing outside his house. Irfan tried to signal to him to go back inside the house but Babloo called out to Tabish. They had a previous account to settle. Tabish owed Babloo some money. Babloo was curious to know what was going on between Shakib, Irfan and Tabish, and asked Tabish to forget about the previous account. He pulled out a joint from his pocket, rolled it into a cigarette, and the three of them smoked it. Tabish and Babloo were friends once again.

Babloo left for his room before Shakib arrived on his bike. Shakib took Irfan to his room and asked Tabish to be ready. The three again went to the spot, but Shehla was already leaving in her car as they reached her house. They decided to execute the murder in the evening the same day.

In the evening, Tabish and Irfan reached the spot and waited for Shehla outside her house. It was dark and drizzling, the best time to do the deed, they thought. They would pounce upon her the moment she stepped out of her car and finish the entire story. Around 9.15 p.m., Shakib called and asked them to leave the spot, saying that Shehla had gone somewhere and there was no point waiting for her.

On 16 August 2011, Irfan and Tabish reached the pre-decided spot near Hotel Palace in Shahjahanabad on a black Pulsar motorbike at 8.25 a.m. Shakib left his Nishatpura house after 8.45 a.m. As he reached the meeting spot at 9.31 a.m., all three got into Shakib's car and discussed their plan for the last time. Shakib asked Irfan to check the .315-bore countrymade gun that he had given him. He ensured that one bullet was properly loaded, while he carried three bullets safely in his pocket. At 9.59.06 a.m., Shakib left the spot in his car, while Tabish riding the bike and Irfan riding pillion left on the black bike. They reached Koh-e-Fiza at 10.11.48 a.m. Tabish parked the bike at a distance of about fifty metres on the road in front of Shehla's house. Tabish took his position on the bike, while Irfan went closer to the main gate, trying to look inside the house. Shehla's Santro car was parked next to the boundary wall in its usual position.

Shakib reached Koh-e-Fiza at 10.15 a.m. He parked his car on the road across the empty space in front of the house. He sat inside the car and could clearly see Tabish sitting on his bike, while Irfan walked in front of Shehla's house.

At 10.15.22 a.m., Shakib called Irfan and instructed him to position himself in such a manner that he could see the target walk out from the house. He also asked Irfan to act as though he was talking to someone on his phone.

Irfan moved a little further away from the house, but he did not know whom to call to act as though he was busy on the phone.

At 10.18.23 a.m., Shakib called Irfan again. He was annoyed. 'Any passer-by can ask what you are doing in front of the house.

Give an impression that you are talking to someone on the phone. Or at least give an impression that you are trying someone's number. Call 367; it's a toll-free number. Keep dialling it again and again. Keep doing this while your eyes are on the main gate,' he instructed.

While talking to Shakib, Irfan had walked to the corner of the road. He took his position in front of the house once again and dialled the toll-free number, 367, for the first time on that day at 10.22.55 a.m. The toll-free number gave the complete information about the account balance in twenty-five seconds, but he disconnected the phone in 20.6 seconds. At 10.23.20 a.m., he dialled the number again and this time the call lasted for 23.6 seconds. At 10.24.32 a.m., he called a Reliance GSM UP East number; this call lasted for 198.1 seconds.

At the end of this call, he again started dialling 367. He waited till the call neared completion and then dialled again. In between these calls, he would come close to the main gate of Shehla's house and would then walk back towards the pole from where he could see the gate. He had already made more than twenty-five calls to 367, when Shakib called again. The call lasted for twelve seconds and his only instruction was to stay cool. Shakib once again assured Irfan that he would get the money if he did the job properly.

Irfan made twenty-four more calls to 367 till 11.13.20 a.m. At 11.14.17 a.m., he got a call from Shahid. The call lasted 30.3 seconds. Ten seconds after this call, Irfan dialled 367 yet again.

On the other end of the open ground outside Shehla's house, Shakib remained seated in his car. He rolled up his windows and kept a watch on both Tabish and Irfan.

At around 11.19 a.m., Shehla walked out of her house towards her car, opened the door, sat in the driver's seat, and was about to put the car keys in the ignition, when Irfan pounced on her from the rear side and shot her in the trachea. Immediately after pumping the bullet in Shehla, Irfan rushed towards Tabish and the two sped away. Shakib saw them flee the spot.

At 11.19.28 a.m., Shehla's associate Arpit called her on her phone, when she was taking her last breaths. She was dead within the next few minutes.

After fleeing from the scene of crime, Tabish and Irfan headed back towards the hotel in Shahjahanabad, the spot where they had gathered in the morning. At 11.22.33 a.m., they had reached the Idgah Hills area, when Shakib called to inquire if the task was accomplished. The call lasted for ten seconds and Irfan confirmed that he had done the job. Shakib waited for the next four minutes to see what was happening outside the house, and then, at 11.26.46 a.m., called up Zahida. He could not wait any further to break the news to her. 'Mubarak ho sahib. This time we did it in front of her house. She has been shot dead…' The call lasted forty-two seconds.

Zahida, who was at her office in MP Nagar, was ecstatic. Her happiness knew no bounds. She immediately asked her employee Rohit to go to Shehla's office and see if her car was there. After Rohit confirmed that the car was not there, Zahida sent a message to Sabah on her mobile at 11.30 a.m. 'The job has been done,' she wrote in the text message.

Sabah called back from her number on the number from which she had received the message. The call lasted 203 seconds. The two friends discussed in detail about their future course of action. The two also decided to meet immediately.

After talking to Shakib from Idgah Hills, Tabish and Irfan continued riding towards Shahjahanabad. The three met at the spot and from there went to Shakib's house. Shakib asked his two accompliccs to rest at his house and left to collect the money from Zahida. He had already called Zahida and had asked her to meet him near the post office in Shahjahanabad. She came in a black-coloured Indica Vista car. Shakib thought she would hug him, but she did not even get out of her car as she handed over a bundle of notes to him. Shakib reached his Nishatpura home at around 2.00 p.m. and gave Rs 5,000 to Irfan and asked him to leave Bhopal immediately. He advised him to take a bus up till Vidisha, from where he could take a train to Kanpur. He also told him that he would get the remaining money after a few days.

Outside Shehla's house, the scene had turned chaotic. When Shehla's father realized that his daughter had been shot dead, his screams were heard by their neighbour Pushpa Jain, who, at 11.25.32 a.m., called the emergency number 108.

Arpit, Shehla's associate, who lived in the same lane, also rushed to the spot after she stopped taking calls after 11.19 a.m. Realizing that she was dead, he called up an RSS activist, who ran two NGOs. The RSS activist within minutes called up Auntie who was in Delhi. Even before Dohre from the police control room had started calling senior police officers to inform them about the murder, Auntie had called up Bhopal SSP Adarsh Katiyar, informing him about the murder. Before calling Katiyar, she had called up a DSP of the crime branch, asking him to confirm if the news was correct. Between 11.35 a.m. and 12.07 p.m., Auntie and her team had reasons to believe that Darbar was involved.

And then at 12.07 p.m., I had gotten the call that brought the news of the murder of Shehla Masood. 'Just check out why Darbar has got Shehla Masood killed. She has been shot outside her house. She is dead. I'm sorry.'

Fifteen

The Judgement

The courts in Indore remain closed on Saturdays but special CBI judge Balraj Kumar had decided to work on 28 January 2017. Police moved in to set up a barricade about fifty metres from the CBI court at around 9.30 a.m. The on-duty policemen frisked everyone going in and only lawyers and journalists were allowed inside. The judge arrived at around 10.00 a.m. and went straight to his chamber.

By 11.00 a.m. the court premises was buzzing with activity. Five years, five months and eleven days after RTI activist Shehla Masood was shot dead outside her house in Bhopal, the court of special CBI judge Balraj Kumar was all set to pronounce the judgement.

The accused came in three batches. The first to arrive was Irfan, the man who according to the charge sheet filed by the CBI had shot Shehla from point-blank range. Irfan had turned approver during the trial. He corroborated the murder story weaved together by the CBI but there was one major glitch.

In the approver statement made under Section 164 of the Criminal Procedure Code, Irfan said it was not him who pulled the trigger. This was at variance with the initial charge sheet filed by the CBI but during trial the prosecution claimed fresh evidence had surfaced that suggested Irfan was stating the truth. The defence was banking on this changed stance and hoped for an eviction because of lack of evidence.

Tabish arrived along with his cousin Shakib Danger in the second police van that came from the Indore Central Jail. The two were held together in a single handcuff that was held by a policeman at the other end. Shakib posed for the waiting cameras and said what his body language seemed to scream. 'I'm hopeful of an eviction. There is no evidence against us,' he said to the jostling reporters as the two were pushed to the room where undertrials are made to wait till their turn comes in court.

The last to come were Zahida and Sabah, the two friends who were lodged in the jail at Ujjain. The van from the jail stood right in front of the special CBI court but only a lady police officer came out. It was already 12.30 p.m.

The media and lawyers had already taken their seats inside the courtroom by this time. The courtroom was already packed and there was not an inch to stand. Around 12.45 p.m. there was a commotion outside the van again. Photographers pushed each other as Zahida and Sabah stepped out for the first time. Outside, the mercury was soaring.

The lawyers had already started predicting a post-lunch verdict. Everyone thought the judgement would be delivered in the second half as the judge was still busy with his reader inside his chamber. At 1.00 p.m., as some lawyers moved out for lunch, making way for journalists standing at the gate, Judge Balraj Kumar walked into the courtroom.

Outside the courtroom, relatives of all the accused stood in the veranda. The police had formed a human chain on both sides from the jail van to the courtroom gate. Irfan almost ran inside while the remaining four accused shared glances with their relatives. All of them had been given the hope of an acquittal, for lack of evidence.

The defence lawyers had spoken to the media all along narrating how the CBI had failed to piece together a foolproof story. 'The CBI could never recover the weapon of offence. The one which was recovered turned out to be fake. It was not used in the crime as it did not have the signature of the bullet that was recovered from the girl who was killed,' advocate Shrivastava who represented Sabah told the media minutes before his client was ushered inside the courtroom along with Zahida.

Zahida's lawyer spoke of the future. 'Whatever may be the judgement, the losing side will go in appeal. If we do not get justice here, we will go to the high court,' he said. 'This case so far has been fought in the media, so none of the accused ever since they were arrested on 28 February 2012 got bail. Inside the court we stand a very good chance,' he added.

Shakib and Tabish were last to be ushered in. They stood next to the door, surrounded by policemen from all sides. The judge was turning the pages with his eyes firmly fixed on what he was about to announce.

There was absolute silence. No one from Shehla's side could be seen inside the courtroom. Her father had recently suffered a second heart attack and instead waited for the verdict from his bed at his home in Bhopal. Shehla's sister Ayesha, who was in the US, had been up the whole night. She had been calling up journalists every half-hour, asking them what the court had said. Shehla's cousin Rajil too was restless, calling up his media contacts from Dubai, from where he now ran his own hospitality business.

Zahida was the first to be called out by the judge as he continued to look into his papers. As Zahida marked her presence, he looked up and said, 'Convicted under Section 302 read with 120 B of the Indian Penal Code and sentenced for life in jail.' Someone started crying outside the courtroom. There were a few murmurs inside as the judge moved on and called for Sabah. He pronounced, 'Convicted for murder under Section 302 read with 120 B of the Indian Penal Code and sentenced for life in jail.'

Shakib by this time knew his fate. He held on to Tabish as the judge announced their conviction. He tried saying something but the arrogance that he had shown on arrival inside the court premises was gone.

The judge made one last statement, 'Irfan has been acquitted as he had turned approver in the case. A copy of the detailed judgement will soon be handed over to the concerned parties.' He rose from his chair and went back to his chamber again.

It was all over in fifteen minutes. At 1.15 p.m. I called up the assignment desk at India Today, and broke down the relevant portions of the judgement that could now be flashed as breaking news.

The news somehow did not make it to the national headlines. News channels were busy dealing with another developing story that day. No one seemed to care what happened in the Shehla Masood murder case. The media had moved on.

I wondered at the contrast between then and the day when the news was broken. On 16 August 2011, it had been BREAKING NEWS when I had first called up the CNN-IBN assignment desk around noon and blurted out that Shehla Masood – Anna Hazare supporter and RTI activist – had been shot dead outside her house by unidentified assailants. Back then, nobody wanted to miss even the tiniest detail about the case. Indeed, the frenzy and machinations of the media and the police was the stuff potboilers are made of.

'Why was she killed?' I asked Inspector Nayyar, one of the most important members of the team, and a person who had worked tirelessly and selflessly on the case. 'She was killed for nothing,' he said as he pulled me in for a hug.

Bibliography

Bhopal architect got Shehla Masood killed: https://www.youtube.com/watch?v=kICcCdKmRjk

CBI charge sheet in the Shehla Masood murder case: https://www.news18.com/blogs/india/hemender-sharma/killed-for-nothing-cbi-chargesheet-in-shehla-masood-murder-case-11295-746850.html

Government should take Shehla's murder seriously: Jairam Ramesh, *People's Samachar*, Bhopal, 18 August 2011

Information martyr: https://www.outlookindia.com/magazine/story/information-martyr/278127

IPS officer behind RTI activist's murder: https://www.news18.com/blogs/india/hemender-sharma/killed-for-nothing-cbi-chargesheet-in-shehla-masood-murder-case-11295-746850.html

Love and murder in Bhopal: https://www.indiatoday.in/magazine/the-big-story/story/20120514-shehla-masood-murder-bjp-mla-dhruv-narayan-singh-zahida-love-triangle-758319-2012-05-04

MP government recommends a CBI probe: https://www.youtube.com/watch?v=zC_47E1gmw8

Mystery behind Shehla Masood's murder deepens: http://www.im4change.org/latest-news-updates/mystery-behind-shehla-masoods-murder-deepens-by-hemender-sharma-9690.html

New twist in the Shehla murder case: https://www.youtube.com/watch?v=i9yISwOKYOQ

RTI Activist shot dead in Bhopal, *Hindustan Times*, Bhopal, 17 August 2011

Shanu Olanga: https://inextlive.jagran.com/shanu-olanga-murdered-exclusive-photos-201112040002

Shehla's death: murder or suicide? *Dainik Bhaskar*, Bhopal, 17 August 2011

Shehla Masood murder: evidence tampered with? https://www.ndtv.com/india-news/shehla-masood-murder-evidence-tampered-with-466857

The life and death of Shehla Masood: http://archive.indianexpress.com/news/the-life-and-death-of-shehla-masood/848087/

What really happened to Shehla Masood? https://www.thenational.ae/world/asia/what-really-happened-to-shehla-masood-1.425820

Who killed Shehla Masood? https://www.youtube.com/watch?v=HuPXlvJjClk

Acknowledgements

Mr Rasheed Kidwai, without whose constant prodding and guidance this book would not have been possible. Thank you, sir!

Mr Masood Sultan, Ms Ayesha Jamil and brother Rajil, I owe a lot to you. Without your support, this book was impossible.

Thank you to:

My gurus Professor Vepa Rao, Mr John Dayal and Mr Rajdeep Sardesai, for shaping my journalism.

Mr Sanjay Bragta and Mr Samar Bhandral for providing me shelter in Delhi. Without your support, the journalism dream would have ended in incubation.

My present and past bosses Ziya H Rizvi, Seema Mustafa, Askari Zaidi, Arup Ghosh, Shireen Sethi, Ajeet Sahi, Prashant Tandon, Vinay Tewari, Arnab Goswami, Rahul Kanwal and Supriya Prasad Sir, for believing in my journalism.

R Radhakrishnan Nair – our beloved Radha Sir at CNN-IBN – who left us for a better world in November 2018.

Mr Abid Shah, Mr Sanjay Kaw, Mr ND Sharma, Mr Rakesh Dixit and Mr Bhupendra Chaubey, for their never-ending support.

A big thank you to my friends Satinath Sarangi, Rachna Dhingra, Deshdeep Saxena, Deepak Tiwari, Brajesh Rajpoot, Rakesh Agnihotri, Ranjan Shrivastava, and Shamsher Chandel, who were always present with the right advice at the right time.

Sincere thanks to Dalip Vishwakarma, my go-to man at CNN-IBN, who kept all the papers in order. Thanks to colleagues Sharad Kapoor, Pankaj Dwivedi and Irshad Khan for their support too.

My mom and my brother Goverdhan, for taking care of things back home. My mom-in-law, for coming to our rescue whenever required, and dad-in-law, for not letting go of his cheer when we made such demands of him.

Rohini, Swati and Vikrant, for providing encouragement.

Mr Kanishka Gupta and Mr Atul Thakur: thank you for all that you did to make this book happen.

Ms Prema Govindan and HarperCollins India, for seeing this book through.

Syed Zaffar, for reinforcing my trust in humanity.

Manoj Sharma, a big thank you to you for your support and guidance in times of crisis.

Sincere thanks to all the named and unnamed sources in the CBI.

Lastly, and most importantly, gratitude to my daughter Navya and my wife Savita who fill my life with love and laughter. They make this life worthwhile and my universe complete.

www.ingramcontent.com/pod-product-compliance
Ingram Content Group UK Ltd.
Pitfield, Milton Keynes, MK11 3LW, UK
UKHW041630190726
13854UKWH00006B/2400

9 789353 029630